T0360845

Absolute Essentials of Strategic Marketing

Strategic marketing is a complex topic, and this short-form textbook illuminates its fundamental elements to provide a bird's-eye view of the field for students of marketing strategy.

Focused on the marketing of goods and services, the book highlights how incremental changes in the market environment drive changes to marketing strategies. The author, an experienced marketing expert, uses the concept of 'strategic windows' to facilitate student understanding, looking at how firms can best anticipate and react to opportunities and threats.

Enhanced by text features such as essential summaries, focused references and additional online supplements, this very short introduction enables the reader to zero in on the core priorities for strategic marketers. The result is a volume that is valuable reading for marketing students around the world.

Tony Proctor is Emeritus Professor in Marketing at the University of Chester, UK.

Absolute Essentials of Business and Economics

Textbooks are an extraordinarily useful tool for students and teachers, as is demonstrated by their continued use in the classroom and online. Successful textbooks run into multiple editions, and in endeavouring to keep up with developments in the field, it can be difficult to avoid increasing length and complexity.

This series of shortform textbooks offers a range of books which zero-in on the absolute essentials. In focusing on only the core elements of each sub-discipline, the books provide a useful alternative or supplement to traditional textbooks.

Titles in this series include:

Absolute Essentials of Operations Management
Andrew Greasley

Absolute Essentials of Strategic Management
Barry J. Witcher

Absolute Essentials of Green Business
Alan Sitkin

Absolute Essentials of Entrepreneurship
Nerys Fuller-Love

Absolute Essentials of Strategic Marketing
Tony Proctor

For more information about this series, please visit: www.routledge.com/ Absolute-Essentials-of-Business-and-Economics/book-series/ABSOLUTE

Absolute Essentials
of Strategic Marketing

Tony Proctor

LONDON AND NEW YORK

First published 2021
by Routledge
2 Park Square, Milton Park, Abingdon, Oxon OX14 4RN

and by Routledge
605 Third Avenue, New York, NY 10017

Routledge is an imprint of the Taylor & Francis Group, an informa business

Copyright © 2021 Tony Proctor

The right of Tony Proctor to be identified as author of this work has been asserted by him in accordance with sections 77 and 78 of the Copyright, Designs and Patents Act 1988.

British Library Cataloguing-in-Publication Data
A catalogue record for this book is available from the British Library

Library of Congress Cataloging-in-Publication Data
A catalog record for this book has been requested

ISBN 13: 978-0-367-43775-6 (hbk)

Typeset in Times New Roman
by Apex CoVantage, LLC

Visit the eResources: http://www.routledge.com/9780367437756

Contents

Preface

There are many definitions of strategy, but in business it refers to how a firm sets about both setting and achieving organizational objectives. In this book we look specifically at marketing strategy, and in particular the strategy concerning the formulation and implementation of the marketing mix. The successful implementation of the marketing mix leads to satisfaction of customer wants and needs and increases the likelihood of achieving an organization's objectives in the marketplace. In recent years, relationship marketing has come to the fore as strategic alliances and networks involving firms working together towards shared goals has become more fashionable. The strategic management of such relationships is at the core of relationship marketing. The argument put forward in this book is that when changes in the market and the marketing environment are incremental in nature, firms can successfully adapt themselves to the new situation by modifying current marketing and other functional programmes.

However, if the cumulative changes in the economic, technological, social, political and cultural environments remain unnoticed by a company's managers until it is too late to respond, the problems which they create for the firm may be overwhelmingly difficult to overcome. Similarly, when the degree of market change is of such magnitude that the competence of a firm to continue to compete effectively is questioned, then the firm may be experiencing the closure of an important *strategic window*. Where change, leading eventually to the closure of a strategic window, is either very rapid or very slow the consequences may well be disastrous. In the first case, the window closes before an organization can respond and, in the second instance, it does not even notice that the window is about to close until it is too late to respond.

It is important to examine not only where the firm is today but how well equipped it is to deal with tomorrow. In particular, the task of predicting non-incremental changes in the market is of critical importance. Existing firms and their competitors can sometimes be replaced in a comparatively short space of time by a whole new range of competitors. Firms which are oblivious to the opening and closing of strategic window, firms which fail to utilize overlapping strategic windows to best advantage or firms which are unable to divest when a window closes risk disaster.

The book looks at many of the issues indicated above. It sets out a framework for organizations to follow in order to meet any threats they may encounter and make the best of opportunities that may occur in the marketing environment.

Tony Proctor
2020

Introduction

This is a very short introduction to strategic marketing. It is comprehensive in nature and provides pointers to key aspects of the subject. You will be provided with an overview of an important aspect of business strategy. In practice strategy may be formally planned and implemented or evolve and develop over time. This has to be borne in mind when reading about the subject. However, to make the subject matter clearer and readily understandable the subject has to be presented in a logical and structured manner. The pedagogical features of the book include essential summaries, focused references/readings and online supplements to help achieve this objective.

There are many definitions of strategy, but in business it refers to how a firm sets about both setting and achieving organizational objectives. In this book we look specifically at strategies relating to the marketing of goods and services. The argument put forward in this book is that when changes in the market and the marketing environment are incremental in nature, firms can successfully adapt themselves to the new situation by modifying current marketing and other functional programmes.

Such changes in the environment can be introduced through technological innovations, changes in customer tastes, changes in legal regulations, economic and financial constraints or any changes in environmental conditions. In addition the nature of competition may also change, and in particular the elements which make up the five forces of Porter's competition model. New entrants to the industry may appear; substitute products may become more attractive propositions to customers; both suppliers and customers may find their bargaining powers strengthened; and the balance of competition power between the incumbent firms in the industry may change as one firm develops a competitive advantage. However, if all these changes remain unnoticed until it is too late to respond, the problems which they create for the firm may be overwhelmingly difficult to overcome.

Organizations need to:

1   Identify the opportunities and threats posed by the opening and closing of strategic windows.
2   Analyze all the relevant internal and external environmental factors acting upon the firm in the context of the strategic windows.
3   Determine the best strategy or set of strategies that are likely to enable the firm to take best advantage of the strategic window while it is open.
4   Ensure that adequate resources are available to implement the chosen strategies.
5   Implement the chosen strategy to take best advantage of the opportunities presented by the strategic window and to minimize the risks posed by the threats.

In this book we will be systematically working through the process. It is the opening and shutting of strategic windows and how the firm might react to this that is the topic of interest. We discuss the nature and formulation of business and marketing strategy and point to the need for strategic marketing management in order to carry it out. We also outline the nature of the marketing management process that is involved.

The organization has to keep abreast of developments in its external and internal environments. It also has to ensure that a matching process between skills and resources is available to take best advantage of developments and opportunities in the environment and to avoid any threats that are posed. We look at the resources that the firm has available and at the developments in the environment that can take place that lead to opportunities and threats with which the firm has to get to grips. An analysis of the relevant factors which impinge on the opening and shutting of strategic windows needs to be undertaken by an organization prior to making strategic decisions.

1 Marketing strategy

The essence of strategy

Strategy can apply at all levels in an organization and pertain to any of the functional areas of management. At its simplest, strategy is a plan of action to achieve a major or overall aim. By contrast, a tactic is an action or strategy carefully planned to achieve a specific end (The New Oxford Dictionary of English, Oxford University Press). In the context of marketing there may be pricing, product, promotion, distribution, marketing research, sales, advertising, merchandising etc. strategies. All these are related to promoting the organization's aim to satisfy customers specific wants and needs.

The marketing strategy in relationship to overall corporate strategy

The corporate strategy of an organization defines the overall plan relating to the organizations, goals, policies, decisions and sequences of action. In the simplest case, the marketing strategy of the organization integrates with the corporate strategy to achieve the overall objectives of an organization. More complex organizations may comprise separate business units, each of which has its own overall strategy related to the corporate strategy for the organization. In this case the marketing strategy for each business unit is related to the individual business unit's overall strategy.

Marketing strategy considerations

When setting strategy there is a need to consider:

Stakeholder interests and values

Stakeholders are held to be those individuals or groups that have a 'stake' in the organization. Stakeholders include customers, employees, management, stockholders, creditors, suppliers, community and sometimes even competitors (Carroll, 1993). Stakeholder interests and values are important considerations when considering strategic decisions (viz. Jensen, 2001; Bryson, 2004). Their interests vary from firm to firm according to the industry and the markets that are served by the firm. Interests include how factors such as product/service development and delivery, promotional mix, support services, manufacturing and production processes, R&D and material purchasing affect the stakeholders:

1 Customers: Their wants and needs and how political, economic, sociocultural and technological influences all impact upon the nature of customer wants and needs.
2 Competition: How to position the firm competitively in the minds of its customers so that its products and services stand out very favourably in important respects in relationship to competitors.
3 Product life cycles: How different stages in the life cycle of products (and their markets and industries in which they are placed) have ramifications for marketing strategy. Some firms may be suited to exploiting certain types of product market opportunities more than others. Every firm will be not able to exploit the same situation to its advantage. Having the necessary skills and assets, or having access to them, is critical in implementing successful marketing strategies.

Strategic windows

Abell (1978) suggested that there are only limited periods when the fit between the key requirements of a market and the particular competencies of a firm competing in that market is optimum. This constitutes the best conditions for a firm with respect to a strategic window of opportunity. Investment in a product line or a market area should be timed to coincide with periods during which a strategic window is open. Correspondingly, withdrawal should be considered where something which once was a good fit is no longer a good fit. However, when changes in the market and the marketing environment are incremental in nature, firms can successfully adapt themselves to the new situation by modifying current marketing and other functional programming, thereby keeping the strategic window open. Such changes can be introduced through technological innovations, changes in customer tastes, changes in legal regulations, economic and financial constraints or any changes in environmental conditions.

The nature of competition may also change. New entrants to the industry may appear; substitute products may become more attractive propositions to customers; both suppliers and customers may find their bargaining powers strengthened; and the balance of competition power between the incumbent firms in the industry may change as one firm develops a competitive advantage.

However, if the cumulative changes in the economic, technological, social, political and cultural environments remain unnoticed by a company's managers until it is too late to respond, the problems which they create for the firm may be overwhelmingly difficult to overcome (Large, 1992; Johnston et al., 2008). Similarly, when the degree of market change is of such magnitude that the competence of a firm to continue to compete effectively is questioned, then the firm may be experiencing the closure of an important strategic window. Where change, leading eventually to the closure of a strategic window, is either very rapid or very slow, the consequences may well be disastrous.

It is important to examine not only where the firm is today but how well equipped it is to deal with tomorrow. In particular, the task of predicting non-incremental changes in the market is of critical importance. Existing firms and their competitors can sometimes be replaced in a comparatively short space of time by a whole new range of competitors.

Opportunities and threats presented by the opening and closing of strategic windows

Organizations need to:

1   Identify the opportunities and threats posed by the opening and closing of strategic windows.
2   Analyze all the relevant internal and external environmental factors acting upon the firm in the context of the strategic windows.
3   Determine the best strategy or set of strategies that are likely to enable the firm to take best advantage of the strategic window while it is open.
4   Ensure that adequate resources are available to implement the chosen strategies.
5   Implement the chosen strategy to take best advantage of the opportunities presented by the strategic window and to minimize the risks posed by the threats.

The whole idea of strategic marketing is that the organization has to keep abreast of developments in its external and internal environments. It ensures that a matching process between skills and resources is available to take best advantage of developments and opportunities in the environment and to avoid any threats that are posed. The organization has to consider the resources that it has available and look at the developments in the environment that can take place that lead to opportunities and threats with which it has to come to grips.

Competitive strategy

Developing a competitive strategy means developing a broad formula for how a business is going to compete, what its goals should be and what policies will be needed to *attain* those goals. Competitive strategy is a combination of the ends or goals for which the firm is striving and the means or policies by which it is seeking to get there.

A competitive strategy requires the consideration of matters that determine the upper limits of what it can reasonably accomplish. An organization's strengths and weaknesses are reflected in its profile of assets and skills relative to competitors. This profile includes financial resources, technological posture, brand identification and so on. The personal values of an organization are reflected in the motivations and needs of key executives and other personnel who implement strategic decisions. Strengths and weaknesses along with values determine from an internal point of view what competitive strategy a company can successfully adopt.

An organization's industry and broader environment determine its external limits. Societal expectations reflect the impact on the company of such things as government policy, social concerns, evolving mores and many others. All of these factors must be considered before a business can develop a realistic and implementable set of goals and policies. Assessment of the appropriateness of a competitive strategy is achieved by testing the proposed goals and policies for consistency as follows:

Internal consistency

Are the goals mutually achievable?
Do the key operating policies address the goals?
Do the key operating policies reinforce each other?

Environmental fit

Do the goals and policies exploit industry opportunities?
Do the goals and policies deal with industry threats (including competitive response) to the degree possible with available resources?
Does the timing of the goals and policies reflect the ability of the environment to absorb the actions?
Are the goals and policies responsive to broader societal concerns?

Resource fit

Do the goals and policies match the resources available to the company relative to competition?

Does the timing of the goals and policies reflect the organization's ability to change?

Communication and implementation

Are the goals well understood by the key implementers?
Is there enough congruence between the goals and policies and the values of the key implementers to ensure commitment?
Is there sufficient managerial capability to allow for effective implementation?

The strategic process

The strategic process refers to the manner in which strategy is formulated. There are several approaches:

- the rational approach, making use of tools such as SWOT (strengths, weaknesses, opportunities and threats) analysis and portfolio models;
- the flexible approach, which employs multiple scenario planning;
- the creative approach, which reflects the use of imagination in planning;
- the behavioural approach, which reflects the influence of power, politics and personalities; and finally,
- the incremental approach, which is based on small adjustments or changes to previously successful strategies.

Process for formulating a competitive strategy

The process consists of asking:

1   What is the business doing now? Where are we now?

   Identification: What is the implicit or explicit current strategy?
   Assumptions: What assumptions about the company's relative position, strengths and weaknesses, competitors and industry trends must be made for the current strategy to be viable?

2   What is happening in the environment?

   Industry analysis: What are the key factors influencing competitive success? What are the important industry opportunities and threats?
   Competitor analysis: What are the capabilities and limitations of existing and potential competitors, and what are their probable future moves?

Societal analysis: What important government, social and political factors will present opportunities or threats?

Strengths and weaknesses: Given an analysis of industry and competitors, what are the firm's strengths and weaknesses relative to present and future competition?

3   What should the business be doing?

Tests of assumptions and strategy: How do the assumptions embodied in the current strategy compare with the analysis indicated here? How does the strategy meet the tests indicated here?

Strategic alternatives: What are the strategic alternatives, given this analysis? (Is the current strategy one of these?)

Strategic choice: Which alternative best relates the company's situation to external opportunities and threats?

Strategy identification

There are three possible broad areas for consideration. The first is the selection of product markets in which the firm will operate and the question of how much investment should be allocated to each. The second is the development of functional area strategies, and the third is the determination of the bases of sustainable competitive advantage in those product markets.

Product market strategies: Many strategic decisions involve products: which product lines to continue, which to add and which to delete. Markets need to be selected in which a competitive advantage will exist.

Functional area strategies: This development of a business strategy involves the specification of the strategies in functional areas such as sales, brand management, R&D, manufacturing and finance.

Implementation of strategies

The strategic thrusts representing various ways to achieve sustainable competitive advantage can be implemented in a variety of ways. Differentiation, for instance, can be based upon product quality, product features, innovation, service, distribution or even a strong brand name. Low-cost strategies can be based on an experience curve which links cost reduction to cumulative production volume. However, it can also be based on factors such as no-frills products or automated production processes.

An effective strategy needs to involve assets and skills or synergies based on unique combinations of businesses. Thus, identifying which assets, skills and synergies to develop or maintain becomes a key decision.

Exploring strategy

In the remainder of the book we shall explore may of the points raised here in determining and implementing marketing strategy – specifically, determining how well a firm's products and services and the skills and resources of the firm fit the requirements of strategic windows now and in the future (Chapter 2). To do this, account has to be taken of competition and the changing nature of the industries in which the firm operates (Chapter 3) as well as the political, economic, sociocultural, technological, ecological and legal framework which constitutes the marketing environment (Chapter 4). Important considerations also are the nature and behaviour of current and potential customers and their respective numbers in the population which determine the size of the market for the firm's products and services (Chapter 5). The firm has then to understand and choose a basis for obtaining a sustainable competitive advantage in the marketplace *vis-à-vis* its competitors (Chapter 6). Many firms aspire to grow their sales and profits or at least maintain their current ones. Growth strategies (Chapter 7) indicate how this may be achieved. The detail of how firms achieve the specific marketing objectives, segmentation, positioning and targeting of markets (Chapter 8), and the marketing mix strategy (Chapter 9) has then to be focused upon. Looking back to the topic of growth strategies (Chapter 7), market development is seen as a key strategy. International marketing (Chapter 10) represents an important aspect of a possible market development strategy and needs to be considered in some detail. Marketing via the World Wide Web also provides a new dimension to traditional methods of international marketing. Having made these analyses, the firm has then to develop specific plans to achieve strategic objective and implement them effectively (Chapter 11).

Questions

1 Some people view marketing in terms of a decision-making paradigm. How useful is such a perspective when marketing is viewed within the framework offered by strategic windows?
2 Discuss how an organization should set about identifying possible competitive strategies. How might various stakeholder interests impinge on this process?
3 What do you understand by the strategic process? Under what circumstances might each of the methods indicated in the text be used?
4 What kind of threats or opportunities might be presented to a supermarket today by the opening and closing of strategic windows?
5 How might one identify 'overlapping strategic windows'? How might an organization take advantage of the situation they present?

References

Abell, D.F. (1978), 'Strategic Windows', *Journal of Marketing*, 42(2): 21–26.

Bryson, J.M. (2004), 'What to Do When Stakeholders Matter: Stakeholder Identification and Analysis Techniques', *Public Management Review*, 6(1): 21–53.

Carroll, A.S. (1993), *Business and Society*, 2nd edition, Cincinnati, OH: South Western Publishing Company, p. 22.

Jensen, M.C. (2001), 'Value Maximization, Stakeholder Theory and the Corporate Objective Function', *European Financial Management*, 7(3): 297–317.

Johnston, M., Gilmore, A., and Carson, D. (2008), 'Dealing with Environmental Uncertainty: The Value of Scenario Planning for Small to Medium Sized Enterprises', *European Journal of Marketing*, 42(11): 1170–1178.

Large, M. (1992), 'Eco-Mapping: How to Avoid Boiled Frogs', *Management Education and Development*, 23(4): 317–325.

Further reading

Aaker, D.A. (2005), *Strategic Market Management*, New York: John Wiley & Sons.

Camilleri, M.A. (2018), 'Strategic Planning and the Marketing Effectiveness Audit', in Travel Marketing (ed.), *Tourism Economics and the Airline Product: Tourism, Hospitality & Event Management*, Cham: Springer.

Hooley, G., Piercy, N., Nicolaus, B. and Rudd, J. (2017), *Marketing Strategy and Competitive Positioning*, 6th edition, Harlow: Pearson.

Levitt, T. (1960), 'Marketing Myopia', *Harvard Business Review*, 38(4): 45–56.

Piercy, N.F. (2016), *Market-Led Strategic Change: Transforming the Process of Going to Market*, 5th edition, London: Routledge.

Porter, M.E. (1996), 'What Is Strategy?', *Harvard Business Review*, 74(6): 61–78.

2 Product portfolio and marketing capabilities

The product life cycle

In general, product life cycles (Day, 1981) exhibit the following features:

- Products have a finite lifespan.
- The typical product life cycle curve, as reflected in the sales history of a product is 'S' shaped until it eventually levels off. It is at this point that market maturity occurs and when the maturity phase has run its course, a period of decline follows. In general terms, the stages in the life cycle are known as 'introduction, growth, maturity and decline'.
- The life cycle of a product may be prolonged by finding new uses or new users for the product or by getting present users to increase the amount they use.
- During its passage through the life cycle, the average profitability per unit of the product sold at first increases and then eventually begins to decline.

The concept of the product life cycle is shown in Figure 2.1.

The length of the product life cycle

Product life cycles can vary considerably in terms of length. Mars Bars, for example, have been around since the early part of the 20th century, while some women's and men's clothes come in and out of vogue with amazing alacrity. However, fashions come back in vogue again from time to time, and old products are introduced as new ones.

Features of the product life cycle stages

The introductory stage: Losses or at best low profits are experienced often during the introductory stage because sales are low and promotion and distribution costs are relatively high.

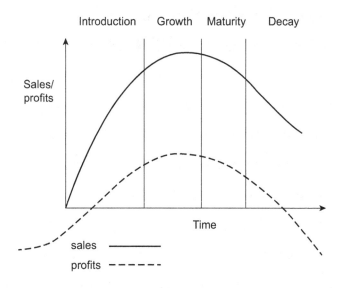

Figure 2.1 The product life cycle

Growth stage: Large profits to be made as the market grows in size and economies of scale come into operation. There is little change in prices and promotional expenditure from the introductory stage.

There is also a decline in the 'promotion to sales ratio'.

The net result of all this is increased profits.

Growth eventually decelerates as fewer first-time buyers enter the market. This often means that a firm has to employ one of several strategies to keep up market growth as long as possible. These include:

* improving product quality,
* adding new features to a product or service,
* refining product styling,
* introducing new models and flanker products,
* entering new market segments,
* greater emphasis on point of sale promotion and
* lowering price to entice price-sensitive buyers.

Maturity stage: The maturity stage follows on from the onset of decline in the rate of sales growth. The latter produces overcapacity in the industry, which in turn leads to increased competition. It is a stage in which profits decline. During the maturity stage, firms implement frequent price reductions and increase advertising and consumer promotions. Emphasis is placed on product research and development to come up with product improvements and flanker brands. While the well-established competitors do well, the weaker competitors may quit the market. Cash earned by strong competitors at this stage can be put into products that are at earlier stages in their life cycles.

Decline stage: Sales of most products eventually start to decline for one or more of several reasons. These include technological progress, shifts in consumer tastes and increased domestic and foreign competition. Overcapacity in the market is produced together with price cutting and lower profits. At this time some firms may withdraw from the market, and those remaining reduce the number of products that they have to offer, pull out of smaller market segments and weaker trade channels, cut the promotion budget or reduce prices even further.

Consideration must be given to dropping products during this stage unless there are good reasons for retaining them.

One problem that has been found in trying to make use of the product life cycle concept as a management tool is that many products do not appear to perform in the marketplace as it suggests. They seem to bypass some stages while getting stuck at other stages. Moreover, as noted, they may even come into vogue again after a period of going out of fashion. These observations have brought about criticisms of the product life cycle as a useful planning tool.

The product/service portfolio

Some products or services produce considerable amounts of cash while others do not. Product portfolio models provide a means of rating products and/or services in order to assess the future probable cash contributions and future cash demands of each product or service.

Portfolio models

Portfolio models are useful diagnostic tools, but more formal and detailed planning mechanisms are required to evolve and evaluate detailed strategies. Portfolio analyses start by examining the positions of products. They consider the attractiveness of the market and the ability of the business to operate competitively within the market. The first of the portfolio models to be used extensively was the growth-share matrix. There have been a number of variations on the portfolio approach, but they all rely on the work of the Boston Consulting Group (BCG) for theoretical and empirical underpinning.

The Boston Matrix: The Boston approach maps products onto a two-dimensional matrix (Henderson, 1970). The method applies equally well to services or any form of strategic business unit. The two axes of the matrix are relative market share and market growth rate.

The concept of the Boston Matrix is shown in Figure 2.2.

One interprets the strength or limitations of a product by its position in the matrix. Products falling into the high growth, high market share quadrant are termed 'stars'. They are tomorrow's cash earners. Being high market share businesses, they will be highly profitable and generate a lot of cash, but at the same time their high growth will also mean that they will require a lot of cash both to finance working capital and to build capacity. Thus, though profitable, stars might have either positive or negative net cash flow.

Products positioned in the low growth, high market share quadrant are designated 'cash cows'. These are the real cash generators, being profitable as a result of their high relative market share. It is quite likely that they will also create surplus cash not required to finance growth.

Products falling into the low growth, low relative market share quadrant are designated 'dogs'. These are inherently unprofitable and seem to possess no future, though their cash requirements are low.

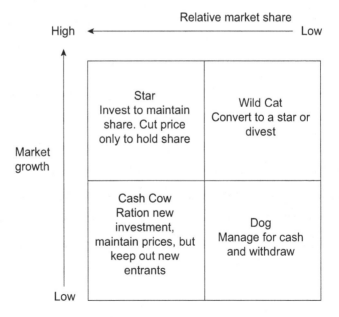

Figure 2.2 The Boston Matrix

Products in the high growth, low market share segment have been referred to as 'wild cats', 'problem children' or simply '?'s. They are unprofitable as a result of their low market share, and they consume a lot of cash merely to maintain their market position because of the high growth rate of the market.

The overall strategy is defined simply with regard to the management of cash flows in order to achieve a balanced portfolio over time. Cash is obtained from cash cows and invested in stars to convert them into tomorrow's cash cows. Dogs are divested and problem children are either converted into stars or liquidated. In this way a balanced portfolio should be achieved with an adequate succession of stars ready to take over from today's cash generators, the cash cows.

While the matrix is intuitively appealing, it had shortcomings which limited its value as an analytical tool. Important ones were:

a   that the BCG ignored products or businesses that were new, and
b   that the BCG overlooked markets with a negative growth rate.

Product life cycle portfolio matrix: To deal with specific criticisms aimed at the BCG matrix, Barksdale and Harris (1982) designed their own matrix. Using the same assumptions as are inherent in the BCG matrix, Barksdale and Harris brought out the additional issues that arise out of introducing new products and products in declining markets. These took the form of:

Warhorses: These are cash cows which develop when an established market enters decline. The products still exhibit a high market share and can still be substantial cash generators. Marketing expenditure may still have to be reduced, or selective withdrawal from market segments or elimination of certain models may still be necessary.

Dodos: Such products possess a low share in declining markets, and there is little opportunity for growth or cash generation. Usually they should be removed from the portfolio, but if competitors are in the course of withdrawing from the market and look as if they will all have withdrawn fairly soon, it may be profitable for 'dodos' to remain.

Infants: These are high risk products not earning profits and using up considerable cash.

As with the BCG there are still problems in defining products and markets or even rates of growth.

The GE/McKinsey matrix: The Boston Matrix and product life cycle portfolio matrix can be difficult to use because both market growth rates and relative market shares may be difficult to measure accurately. A nine-celled multi-factor portfolio matrix was designed by General Electric working with McKinsey & Company to overcome some of the limitations of considering only market share and market growth in accomplishing strategic marketing management. Once again, services or other forms of business unit can be plotted in place of products.

GE originally considered size, market growth, pricing, market diversity and competitive structure as the major factors to describe industry attractiveness. In the case of business strength, attention was focused on size, growth, share, position, profitability, margins, technology position, strength/weaknesses, image, pollution and people. However, a company can use different factors in either the business strength or industrial attractiveness category, depending on the situation.

Although the GE/McKinsey matrix offers a greater number of prescriptions than the Boston Consulting Group matrix, the general outcome is not much different to that produced by the latter. In all cases, products exhibiting a low share of a low growth market should be divested, those with a high share of a low growth market should be milked and those having a high share of a high growth market should receive investment.

The Shell Chemicals Directional Policy matrix is very similar to the GE/ McKinsey matrix. The major differences are greater precision in the assessment of factor ratings together with somewhat more explicit strategy guidelines. Rather than using single measures of success, that is, market growth rate and relative market share, the DPM uses a multivariate approach where market growth rate is replaced by market attractiveness and relative market share by business strength.

Market attractiveness and business strength both comprise a set of critical success factors (CSFs). The content of each of these sets of CSFs depends entirely upon the company and the competitive environment.

Comments on portfolio model usage

Portfolio models are easy to use, and the benefit of using such models is to gain some idea of the profile of strong/weak products or services in the mix. They may, however, cause an organization to put too much stress on market-share growth and entry into high growth businesses. They may also cause firms to pay insufficient attention to managing the current business.

Another problem is that the results produced by using the models are responsive to the weights and ratings and can be manipulated to produce desired results. Since an averaging process is taking place, several businesses may end up in the same cell location but vary considerably in terms of their ratings against specific factors. Moreover, many products or services will end up in the middle of the matrix, and this makes it difficult to suggest an appropriate strategy. The models do not accommodate the synergy between two or more products/services, and this suggests that making decisions for one in isolation from the others may be shortsighted.

Marketing capability analysis

Making the best of a strategic window opportunity not only involves identifying promising opportunities but also having the right kind of resources to make the best of the opportunity. In addition to an analysis of external threats and opportunities in the environment, strategy development must be based on objectives, strengths and capabilities of a business.

Marketing competencies

Market orientation is central to marketing. A firm characterized as market oriented might:

a   appreciate that understanding present and potential customer needs is fundamental to providing superior customer value;
b   encourage the systematic gathering and sharing of information regarding present and potential customers and competitors as well as other related constituencies; and
c   instil an integrated, organization-wide priority to respond to changing customer needs and competitor activities in order to exploit opportunities and circumvent threats.

Market orientation places emphasis on the organization-wide generation and sharing of market intelligence, which produces responsiveness to market needs. Strategy selection must reflect the demands of environmental changes, but at the same time, it should help to develop a company's distinctive competencies. It is through competitive positioning that the benefits from both of these independent approaches are obtained. It enables firms to compete by identifying target markets and encapsulating the competitive advantage that will be sought in trying to reach these target markets. It recognizes that if the advantage is to be sustainable in the face of competition, it has to be based on the firm's distinctive resources and capabilities.

Resource-based view of the firm: For a strategy to be sustainable it has to be based on the firm's resources and capabilities. Organizational assets are the endowments a business has accumulated such as those resulting in scale, plant, location and brand equity, whereas capabilities reflect the synergy between these assets and enable them to be deployed to the company's advantage. Capabilities may be conceptualized as complex bundles of skills and collective learning which promote the coordination of functional activities in an organization (Day, 1994).

Organizational assets comprise things such as: physical assets – land, facilities, buildings, equipment; financial assets – cash, credit rating; operations assets – machinery, systems and processes; human assets – employees, their qualities and skills; marketing assets – distribution penetration, marketing expertise, market positioning, market knowledge, customer loyalty, brand name, reputation, relationships with distributors; legal assets – patents and copyrights; systems – management information systems and decision support mechanisms. Company capabilities refer to a firm's ability to deploy assets through organizational processes to achieve desired results. Both this approach and marketing competences are required to ensure strategic success.

Assessing competitive advantage

The value chain: Porter (1985) considered the value chain as a means of ascertaining the competitive advantage that a firm might possess. A value chain of this nature comprises two types of value-creating activities:

Primary value activities

inbound logistics – material handling and warehousing;
operations – transforming inputs into the final product
outbound logistics – order processing and distribution;
marketing and sales – communication, pricing and channel management; and
service – installation, repair and parts.

Secondary value activities

procurement – procedures and information systems;
technology development – improving product and processes/systems;
human resource management – hiring, training and compensation; and
firm infrastructure – general management, finance, accounting, governmental relations and quality management.

Each of the activities in the value chain is a potential source of competitive advantage and thus should be considered in undertaking self-assessment.

Sales and profitability: A reasonably sensitive measure of what customers think about a product or service is its sales or market share. If customers alter their views about a product or service, sales and market share should be affected. Increased sales can mean that a customer base has grown. Increased share can provide the potential to gain a strategic competitive advantage in the form of economies of scale and experience curve effects. The converse is also true when sales decline. Nevertheless, a difficulty with using sales as a measure is that it can be influenced by short-term promotional activities on the part of the firm or its competitors. An analysis of sales or share should therefore be viewed within the context of a study of customer satisfaction.

Non-financial performance assessment: Many factors, however, will be of a non-financial nature. Innovation, quality, customer relations, management capabilities, alliances, technology, brand value, employee relations, environmental and community issues taken together are important value creation drivers in an organization. Monitoring and assessing these are important. Interest has developed in recent years on how performance and can best be measured and reported to management. This has led to the development of interest in measuring performance against goals. The 'balanced scorecard' (Kaplan and Norton, 1996) has been adopted widely for this use.

A balanced scorecard is a performance measurement technique that strikes a balance between financial and non-financial/operating measures, relating performance to rewards and taking into account the multiplicity of stakeholder interests. The balanced scorecard examines the organization from four perspectives and requires one to develop metrics, collect data and analyze it relative to each of these perspectives:

- The Learning and Growth Perspective
- The Business Process Perspective
- The Customer Perspective
- The Financial Perspective

Use of the scorecard helps give a clear picture as viewed from different perspectives. Performance measures enable improvements to be identified. These measures relate to characteristics of products, services, processes and operations and portray the factors that lead to improved customer, operational, and financial performance.

It is difficult to create performance indicators that really reflect long-term prospects. Attention should be placed on assets and skills that underlie current and future strategies and their strategic competitive advantages. Such measures might include customer satisfaction, brand loyalty measures, product or service quality measures, brand or firm associations, relative cost, new product activity and manager–employee capability and performance.

Questions

1 Discuss the usefulness of the concept of the product life cycle as a planning tool. What are its major weaknesses?
2 Explain why firms need to have a balanced product/service portfolio with elements at different stages in the product life cycle to ensure long-term survival and growth.

3   What are the limitations of portfolio matrices such as these described in the chapter? How useful are they to marketers?
4   How would the various kinds of self-appraisal that a firm could undertake be used in the course of formulating strategies? Examine each aspect of self-appraisal in detail.
5   How might you apply 'value chain analysis' in each of the following types of organization?

   a   A university
   b   A hospital

References

Barksdale, H.C. and Harris, C.E. (1982), 'Portfolio Analysis and the Product Life Cycle', *Journal of Long-Range Planning*, 15(6): 35–64.

Day, D.S. (1981), 'The Product Life Cycle: Analysis and Applications Issues', *Journal of Marketing*, 45(4): 60–67.

Day, G.S. (1994), 'The Capability of Market Driven Organizations', *Journal of Marketing*, 58(3): 37–52.

Henderson, B.D. (1970), 'The Product Portfolio', in *The Boston Consulting Group Perspectives No. 66*, Boston, MA: Boston Consulting Group.

Kaplan, R.S. and Norton, D.P. (1996), 'Using the Balanced Scorecard as a Strategic Management System', *Harvard Business Review*, 74(1): 75–85.

Porter, M.E. (1985), *Competitive Advantage*, New York: The Free Press.

Further reading

Cacciolatti, L. and Lee, S.H. (2016), 'Revisiting the Relationship between Marketing Capabilities and Firm Performance: The Moderating Role of Market Orientation, Marketing Strategy and Organisational Power', *Journal of Business Research*, 69(12): 5597–5610.

Cooper, R.G., Edgett, S.J. and Kleinschmidt, E.J. (2002), *Portfolio Management for New Products*, Cambridge, MA: Perseus Publishing.

Fairbanks, S. and Buchko, A. (2018), 'The Strategic Market Portfolio Matrix Tool', in *Performance-Based Strategy*, Bingley: Emerald Publishing Limited, pp. 101–119.

Kim, N., Shin, S. and Min, S. (2016), 'Strategic Marketing Capability: Mobilizing Technological Resources for New Product Advantage', *Journal of Business Research*, 69(12): 5644–5652.

Mohajan, H. (2017), 'An Analysis on BCG Growth Sharing Matrix', *International Journal of Business and Management Research*, 2(1): 1–6.

Takata, H. (2016), 'Effects of Industry Forces, Market Orientation, and Marketing Capabilities on Business Performance: An Empirical Analysis of Japanese Manufacturers from 2009 to 2011', *Journal of Business Research*, 69(12): 5611–5619.

3 Industry and competition

Industry

Arguably a firm's competitive environment is the industry in which it operates. A key strategic consideration is understanding the structure of the industry – size, growth, competitive structure, cost structure, channels, trends and key success factors (Aaker, 2005) – and what external and internal environmental factors are likely to cause these to change over time. Here we look at some of the factors and how they may have an impact.

Industry life cycle

Like products industries have a life cycle. The concept of an industry life cycle is shown in Figure 3.1.

We distinguish between three stages in the life cycle.

Emerging and developing industries: Emerging industries are either newly formed or reformed industries that have been produced by technological innovations, shifts in cost relationships, emergence of new consumer needs, or other economic and sociological changes that make a new product or service a potentially viable business opportunity (Porter, 1980). In such a situation, there are no preconceived ideas on how to operate competitively.

Maturing industries: Maturity does not occur at any fixed point in development. It can be delayed by innovations or other events that maintain continued growth, and strategic breakthroughs may even lead mature industries to recover rapid growth. Industries can experience more than one transition to maturity. Businesses should try to identify those competitors that do not perceive the need for such changes very clearly or may perceive them but be reluctant to make the often-substantial changes in strategy that are required. Such firms, their markets and customers are obvious targets to attack when formulating marketing strategy. Maintaining growth rate in sales requires that market share has to be increased at the expense of competition. Price

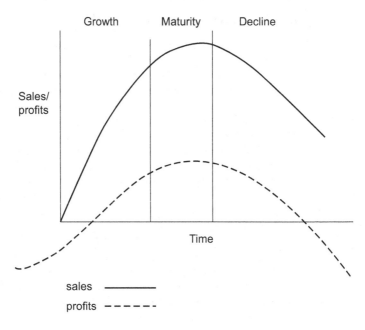

Figure 3.1 The industry life cycle

cutting, new forms of promotional activity and new additional services may be the order of the day.

Customers' attention moves from deciding whether to purchase the product to making choices among brands. Slower growth, more knowledgeable customers and greater technological maturity means that competition is based more upon level of service and cost control. Key questions that the analyst has to answer here relate to responses the firm should make to changes in customer appraisals of the product offerings and suggesting ways of improving customer service and at the same time keeping costs under control.

As growth reaches maturity, *overcapacity* can occur. Scaling down operations or at least careful monitoring of any further demands for increasing capacity may be required. Overcapacity can lead to overproduction and thence to price warfare to take up the production capacity. Forecasting the rate of industry growth and being able to identify turning points and distinguish them from the impacts of recession is of paramount importance.

As the industry progresses through the maturity stage, rationalization of the product mix and correct pricing become key issues and place a considerable amount of emphasis on cost analysis. Emphasis on cost control may accentuate the need to prune and find less risky ways of maintaining market share. At this stage the emphasis may be on trying to get people to buy more of the product, both in terms of amount and frequency of purchase, rather than trying to attract new customers. Sales can often be increased by offering additional services or peripheral equipment or by upgrading and widening the product line. Some degree of diversification of product market scope may result. However, it is a more economical strategy than that of finding new customers since the latter means winning market share, which can be costly.

Declining industries: Declining industries are not as attractive as growing industries to many competitors, and sooner or later scale economies may cause the larger firms to consider withdrawal, thereby leaving an often relatively large market without major forces within it. Moreover, it may be possible for a firm to revitalize an industry. This may be achieved by creating new markets, new products, new applications, revitalized marketing methods, government-assisted growth and/or the exploitation of submarkets. Analysis of the industry in these circumstances has to point to the direction that a firm might take.

Sometimes a dormant industry can be revitalized by a new product that makes existing products obsolete and accelerates the replacement cycle. A new application for a product can stimulate new industry growth. Government-stimulated growth can take the form of tax incentives or legislation giving rise to a new industry or market. Some firms have been successful in declining or mature industries because they have been able to focus on growth sub-areas, pockets of demand that are healthy and even expanding.

Fragmented industries

Many firms compete in industries where no one firm has a significant market share and is able to impose a strong influence over the industry. Small and medium-sized firms are often to be found in such industries. The essential feature of such industries is the absence of a market leader having the power to shape the industry. Fragmented industries occur across a broad section of different types of business.

Overcoming fragmentation represents a very significant strategic opportunity. The rewards can be high because entry costs are low and there tend to be small and relatively weak competitors who offer little in the way of threats or retaliation. Overcoming fragmentation needs an attack on the fundamental economic factors leading to the fragmented structure. Some common approaches include:

- *Creating economies of scale or experience curve benefits* – process innovations may consolidate an industry.

- *Standardizing diverse market needs* – product or marketing innovations can achieve this.
- *Making acquisitions for a critical mass* – making many acquisitions of neighbouring firms can be successful provided that the acquisitions can be integrated and managed.
- *Spotting industry trends early* – in effect this means examining the impact of market drivers such as political, economic, social, technological and business trends as they impact on the industry.

The need to identify strategic groups within industries

A strategic group is comprised of firms within an industry following similar strategies aimed at similar customers or customer groups. (Mascarenhas and Mascarenhas, 2019) identification of strategic groups is fundamental to industry analysis since, just as industries can rise or fall despite the state of the overall business environment, so strategy groups with distinctive competencies can withstand and even defy the general fluctuations within an industry. Understanding the dynamics of existing strategic groups can be productive in understanding their vulnerability to competitive attack.

Competition

Factors influencing competition

No matter how hard a company tries, if it fails to fit into the dynamics of the industry, ultimate success may not be achieved. Porter (1980) sees competition in an industry being governed by five different sets of forces – see Figure 3.2.

Rivalry among competitors: Competition in an industry is more intense if there are many comparable rivals trying to satisfy the wants and needs of the same customers in the same market or market segment. Moreover, competition increases where industry growth is slow, costs are high and there is a lack of product differentiation. High exit barriers from a market or industry contribute to increased competition. Firms may find it difficult to get out of a business because of the relationship of the business with other businesses in which they are engaged. An organization may also have considerable investments in assets which are used for the specific business and for which no valuable other use can be found.

Bargaining power of customers: Customers can exert influence on producers. Where there are a small number of buyers, for example, or a predominant/single buyer, the producer's opportunities for action are limited. In the situation where one customer accounts for a significant proportion of

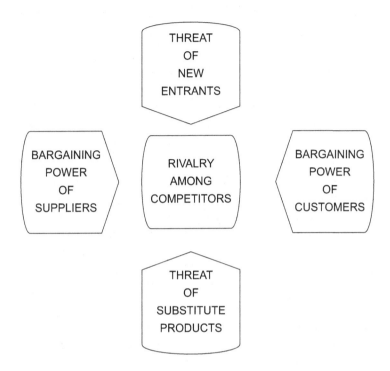

Figure 3.2 The five forces model

a supplier's business, then the one customer can exert considerable influence and control over the price and quality of the products that it buys. Such firms can demand the highest specification in products, with tight delivery times (for just-in-time manufacturing, hence reducing the cost of raw material inventories) and customized products.

In general, the greater the bargaining power of buyers, the less advantage sellers will have. Not all buyers have equal bargaining power with sellers; some may be less sensitive than others to price, quality or service.

Bargaining power of suppliers: Suppliers can exert pressures by controlling supplies. A powerful supplier is in a position to influence the profitability of a whole industry by raising prices or reducing the quality of the goods it supplies. A firm that has few or only one potential supplier may exert little influence over the prices it pays for brought-in materials and components. It may also experience difficulty in influencing the quality of its raw materials and resources. If it is the only purchaser and constitutes an important part of the supplier's business, however, it can exert a great deal of influence over both prices and quality. Another form of supplier power is 'lock-in'. This involves making it difficult or unattractive for a customer to change suppliers.

Powerful suppliers can have the same adverse effects upon profitability as powerful buyers. Suppliers can exert bargaining power on participants in an industry by raising prices or reducing the quality of purchased goods and services. Powerful suppliers can thereby squeeze profitability out of an industry unable to recover cost increases in its own prices.

Threat of new entrants: The threat of new entrants can increase competitive activity in a market. Outsiders will be tempted to enter a market or an industry if they feel that the opportunity is sufficiently appealing in terms of profitability and sales. Markets which have grown to a substantial size become potentially attractive to large powerful firms provided that the level of competitive activity enables them to achieve the kind of market share and profits and sales volume they expect.

This provides an incentive for the firms already operating in the market to make the prospects appear less attractive to would-be entrants by increasing the level of competitive activity. For example, lowering price levels would increase the competition between firms within the market, and it might also deter other firms from entering because it would be more difficult to obtain high profitability levels. Much depends, however, on the cost structure of a would-be entrant.

Suppliers may expand downstream, or buyers may move upstream. This can cause increased competition and a likely reduction in margins. Methods to discourage entry include raising the cost of entry into a market. This may be achieved by developing new products through R&D which the competition finds hard to match, introducing new marketing initiatives, such as long-term contracts with customers, or raising the cost of entry through economies of scale.

Threat of substitute products or services: Substitutes, or alternative products that can perform the same function, impose limits on the price that an industry can charge for its products. The presence of substitutes is not obvious and may not be easily perceived by firms operating in an industry. Substitutes may even be preferred by customers and incumbent firms may only be noticed when it is too late to arrest their dominance.

The threat of substitutes depends on technical comparability of substitutes, the relative price of substitutes, the speed of technological development in 'substitute' industries and the cost of switching. Substitute products that deserve the most attention strategically are those that:

1 are subject to trends improving their price-performance trade-off with the industry's product or
2 are produced by industries earning high profits.

These five 'forces' are rather arbitrary, since a sixth force, government regulation, is often the most significant influence in determining the profitability of an industry.

Competitive strategy and profitability

Maximum profitability can, in principle, only be achieved in one of two ways: either by minimizing costs or by maximizing prices. Thus, any useful business strategy must aim to follow one or the other of these aims: to be the lowest-cost producer or the highest-price seller.

Porter (1980) argues that failure to make the choice between cost leadership and differentiation means that a company is 'stuck in the middle', with no competitive advantage. This results in 'poor performance'. Some researchers have even suggested that the most effective strategies for some situations consist of systematic oscillation between cost leadership and differentiation (Gilbert and Strebel, 1988).

When 'focus' was introduced initially as a generic strategy it obscured the simple structure of the model, which argued that profits could be maximized either by achieving lowest costs or highest prices. Competition reduces profits by the introduction of substitutes, new entrants, etc. as suggested by Porter. Moreover, perfect competition erodes profitability perfectly. Minimizing competitions would minimize erosion of profits, and this could be done by focusing on areas of the market where there are the fewest competitors. This in turn is a recommendation for the adoption of the 'focus strategy'.

Strategy typologies

While Porter's typologies represent one important way of looking at how firms behave in the marketplace, there are other ways of looking at what firms do. Various suggestions have been put forward to account for the strategies adopted by firms. A commonly adopted framework is to consider firms according to the role they play in a market. The suggestion is that firms act as:

Leader: The market leader is the enterprise that has the largest market share. Leadership is exercised with respect to price changes, new product introductions, distribution coverage and promotional intensity. Because of their large volume sales, market leaders enjoy the benefits of economies of scale and accumulated experience, which helps reduce costs and bolster profits. Not surprisingly, dominant firms want to stay in the leading position, and this requires them to:

a   find ways of expanding total market demand,
b   protect market share and
c   even increase market share.

The market leader is conscious of economies of scale of operation and is happiest when making inroads into large and substantial markets. Small specialist markets (niches) are not the prime interest of market leaders (Ferrier et al., 2017).

Challenger: These companies aspire to become market leaders, recognizing the benefits of holding such an exalted position. Challengers attack the leader and other competitors in order to try to gain market share. It is uncommon for market challengers to attack the leader directly. They usually try to gain market share by attacking markets in which the smaller and less efficient firms operate. Such markets, of course, do have to be of a substantial size and not be too small or specialized to deter the larger firms.

There are a variety of strategies that challengers can adopt. One strategy is to produce an enormous variety of types, styles and sizes of products including both cheaper and more expensive models (Ferrier et al., 2017).

Follower: Firms which undertake a good deal of innovation often have to recoup massive investment costs. Market followers are able to copy what the leading firms produce and save themselves the burden of massive investment costs. This means that they can operate very profitably at the going price in a market. Such firms will obviously have to forgo the market share which comes from being first into the field.

Providing they can stay cost efficient and obtain a reasonable share of the market, they can survive. Less efficient ones, however, are open to attack from the market challengers.

Market niching: Most industries include smaller firms that specialize in producing products or in offering services to specific sectors of the market, that is, in specific segments. In so doing they avoid the competitive thrusts of the larger firms for whom specialization does not offer attractive economies of scale, that is, the segments are too small to generate the kind of return on investment that the larger firms require. This is a strategy called market niching.

Market niching is a strategy that is not only of interest to small firms but is also of interest to the small divisions of larger companies. The latter firms seek some degree of specialization. In cases where the latter occurs the position of small firms is not quite so secure. From a firm's point of view, an ideal market niche is:

a of sufficient size to be profitable to a firm serving it,
b capable of growth,
c of negligible interest to major competitors and
d a good fit with the firm's skills and resources (Dalgic and Leeuw, 1994).

Understanding competitors' strategies

A firm has to be regularly comparing its products, prices, channels of distribution and promotional methods with those of its competitors in order to ensure that it is not at a disadvantage. In so doing it can also identify areas where it can gain a competitive advantage.

In order to establish a sustainable competitive advantage in the marketplace it is necessary to know and understand the strategies adopted by competitors. It is important to consider how competition will develop in the future and thus to ascertain the focus of the strategies that competitors are pursuing.

Firms need to monitor competition continually. The main need is for information regarding:

- sales,
- market share,
- profit margin,
- return on investment,
- cash flow and
- new investment.

In addition, knowledge of competitors' financial performances is useful.

Such information enables firms to gain comprehensive impressions of their rivals that may be useful in predicting short-term strategies to be adopted by competitors. A knowledge of competitors' specific objectives would be very welcome since these would give clues as to future strategies that competitors are likely to pursue. This kind of information may be difficult to obtain but may be inferred from present or past activities.

Questions

1 Why is it useful to differentiate between industries at the different stages of their life cycles?
2 Discuss the relationship of the industry life cycle to the concept of the strategic window.
3 Discuss the usefulness of Porter's five forces model in helping an organization to develop its business strategies.
4 Porter argues that failure to make the choice between cost leadership and differentiation implies that a company is 'stuck in the middle', with no competitive advantage. How can this point of view be reconciled with the success of those firms which apply both of these strategic thrusts?

5   Differentiate between:

    a   market leader
    b   market challenger
    c   market follower
    d   market nicher

and discuss the various strategies which might be pursued by each one of the four categories.

References

Aaker, D. (2005), *Strategic Market Management*, New York: John Wiley and Sons Inc.

Dalgic, T. and Leeuw, M. (1994), 'Niche Marketing Revisited: Concept, Applications and Some European Cases', *European Journal of Marketing*, 28(4): 39–54.

Ferrier, J.F., Smith, K.G. and Grimm, C.M. (2017), 'The Role of Competitive Action in Market Share Erosion and Industry Dethronement: A Study of Industry Leaders and Challengers', *Academy of Management Journal*, 42(4): 1017–1039.

Gilbert, X. and Strebel, P. (1988), 'Developing Competitive Advantage', in J.B. Quinn, H. Mintzberg and R.M. James (eds.), *The Strategic Process*, Englewood Cliffs: Prentice Hall.

Mascarenhas, B. and Mascarenhas, M. (2019), 'Strategic Groups', in *Business, Oxford Research Encyclopedia*, Oxford, USA: Oxford University Press.

Porter, M. (1980), *Competitive Strategy*, New York: The Free Press.

Further reading

Aithal, P.S. (2017), 'Industry Analysis: The First Step in Business Management Scholarly Research', *International Journal of Case Studies in Business, IT and Education (IJCSBE)*, 1(1): 1–13.

Kim, W.C. and Mauborne, R. (2005), *Blue Ocean Strategy: How to Create Uncontested Market Space and Make the Competition Irrelevant*, Boston: Harvard Business School Publishing.

Madsen, T.L. and Walker, G. (2016), *Modern Competitive Strategy*, 4th edition, New York: McGraw-Hill.

Porter, M.E. (2004), *Competitive Strategy: Techniques for Analysing Industries and Competitors*, New York: The Free Press.

Proctor, T. (2001), 'Corporate Restructuring: The Pitfalls of Changing Industry Structure', *Management Decision*, 39(3): 197–204.

Scherer, F.M. (1996), *Industry Structure, Strategy and Public Policy*, Upper Saddle River, N.J.: Prentice Hall.

4 The marketing environment

The changing nature of social and cultural aspects of consumers

Demography

Demographic and cultural factors make up society-wide influences and changes that can affect the marketing environment. In terms of demographic factors, the following are of interest to marketers:

- population: size, growth rate, distribution by gender, birth rates, death rates, life expectancy;
- density: location, geographical/regional shifts;
- household/family: size, make-up;
- income/wealth distribution; and
- socio-economic groups: occupations, ethnic groups.

These factors change slowly over time and exert powerful effects on the volume and nature of demand for most products and services. Some influences are obvious: the demand for children's products and services will be related to birth rate patterns. The demand for products and services to meet the wants and needs of the elderly will be related to characteristics and trends of an ageing population.

In some countries there has been a slowing down of the birth rate. Along with this, an extension of life expectancy has resulted in a shift in the profile of the population to that of an ageing one. In addition, many changes have taken place in the make-up and size of family households. Fewer marriages and fewer children coupled with an increase in the labour force of married women have changed the basic nature of the family household. Career couples with no children are now quite common and are a target group of interest to many marketers because of their relatively high disposable income.

Another characteristic seems to have been a growth in non-family households. Some of these are made up of single career people, whereas others are made up of divorced or widowed adults. There has also been an increase in single-parent families. These changes in the structure and characteristics of households have had a major effect on the pattern of demand for a wide range of everyday goods and services.

The nature of cultural values

Often, different regions of a country exhibit different buying preference patterns that seem to reflect different cultural and traditional values. In addition, because many towns and cities throughout the world are now very cosmopolitan in nature, it is quite common to find large ethnic groups living in fairly large concentrations in urban areas. These groups have distinct cultural values which are reflected in their buying preference patterns. For example, ethnic minorities make up a very small proportion of the population of the United Kingdom. But in the Greater London area, in the West Midlands and in West Yorkshire it is significantly greater.

Culture is reflected in the prevalent core beliefs and values of people. These beliefs and values are declared in family and friendship relations, in social conventions and rites, in social institutions and in social order itself. They take a long time to change since they are inextricably linked to such things as family upbringing, the education system, national history, religion and a variety of other institutional phenomena.

A variety of secondary beliefs and values which are less durable and more situationally determined are also to be found. For example, while belief in law enforcement may be rooted in core values, attitudes towards private law enforcement and vigilantes reflect secondary values and beliefs. These beliefs are more likely to vary within society and to change over time. They may also be recognizable in subcultures within society. Subcultures evolve for a variety of reasons and commonly involve a grouping of people with common interests, experiences and motivations. Cultures may also be identified with age groupings, regional affiliations, religious or ethnic associations or even situational facets of lifestyle (e.g. students).

From the point of view of international marketing, language is an important aspect of culture which is particularly relevant to marketing communications. Another aspect of culture which has an influence on consumers is religion. Religious beliefs, both at home and abroad, have a major influence on consumer attitudes and purchase behaviour. This is often reflected in the kinds of food that people consume, the drinks they purchase and even their manner of dress. Moreover, even business practices can vary considerably between different areas and countries. (Sagiv and Schwartz, 2007)

Changes in values and attitudes

Attitudes towards credit have changed substantially over the years. Traditionally, credit purchasing was something which people tended to avoid. Indeed, there was at one time a social stigma against purchasing on credit except for major purchases such as homes and cars.

Changes in society's attitudes towards health over a similar period of time have resulted in a multi-million-pound industry developing and the supply of health products and services. People are now more weight conscious, exercise conscious and conscious about their diets. Moreover, smoking, which at one time was considered a social sophistication, is now considered to be anti-social.

The influence of political, fiscal and economic policies

Political and fiscal policies

Governments are in a position to take actions which can substantially alter a company's marketing environment. In the United Kingdom, privatization of the public utilities has created new terms and conditions for their suppliers and subcontractors. The creation of an internal market within the health service has had a substantial impact on the way in which hospitals and other health service units go about their work.

Legislation over such things as labelling, packaging, advertising and environmentalism all have to be taken into account when designing packaging and formulating advertising messages.

Political instability in a country can also have a marked effect on marketing methods used by exporters in accessing that country's markets. Under such circumstances it may be preferable, for example, to sell the license to manufacture the product to a producer in the country concerned for a once-only royalty fee. Licenses may be granted to produce or market goods and services. In the former case, the license relates to know-how. Royalty payments can be one-off payments, or they can be fixed as a percentage of subsequent sales.

The economic cycle

Traditionally, the economy has been considered to follow a cyclical pattern consisting of four stages: boom, recession, slump (depression) and recovery. Various industries, markets and organizations can, of course, break this trend, either demonstrating a decline in growth during a boom or an expansion during a slump.

In each stage of the cycle there are different business patterns. In times of prosperity, consumer spending is high. Organizations normally exploit this by expanding product lines, increasing promotional efforts, expanding distribution and raising prices, on the presumption that consumers are often willing to pay more for well-known and well-established products and have the means to do so.

In times of recession, the purchasing power of consumers declines and may even stagnate when the economy enters into recovery. During a recession, consumers may shift their buying patterns to purchasing more basic, more functional, less expensive products and spend less on non-essential products. This means that decisions on the purchase of luxury items, such as cars or new homes, may be postponed. Not surprisingly, it is the producers and marketers of luxury goods who are most affected by an economic recession. The strategy for marketers during times of recession is usually to reduce prices and prune the size of product lines.

As recovery starts to be felt, consumers start to buy convenience products and higher priced goods and services. Assessing the strength of a recovery is difficult, and organizations have to assess how quickly consumers are making the transition from recession.

Inflation

One of the most difficult phenomena to deal with during the economic cycle is inflation. Inflation is an increase in the general level of prices in an economy that is sustained over time. Inflation has two main causes:

- excess demand beyond the output capacity of the economy to supply goods and services and
- increases in input costs – wages, raw materials and components.

Inflation, produced by rising prices and resulting in reduced consumer buying power, creates problems for the marketer. Not only is uncertainty introduced into the market through the effect of inflation on costs and sales forecasts, but it also makes it difficult to determine the price to charge during the next budgeting period.

Inflation is not welcomed by the business community. It is administratively expensive to constantly change prices in line with inflation, and it can affect a firm's competitive positions in both domestic and foreign markets. High rates of inflation effectively make imports cheaper but make exports more expensive.

These factors impact on consumer confidence (De Boef and Kellstedt, 2004).

The influence of technology

Technological advances and improvements are a feature of modern-day business. The obsolescence of products within a relatively short period from their introduction is commonplace. Moreover, it is increasingly the case that tomorrow's products are no longer news by the time they are put on the market. During the lead time between an announcement of a new product and the time it can be made available to the consumer, competitors may already have announced improved or better versions of the same product.

Organizations which do not react to technological advances which are relevant to the kinds of products they produce run the risk of rapid product obsolescence and going out of business.

Changes in distribution patterns

Growth in car ownership and the trend to a high percentage of husbands and wives both working, together with increasing standards of living, has led to less time being available for shopping plus greater mobility of the shopper. All of these factors led to the need for one-stop shopping facilities and thence to the development of supermarkets to provide this facility. Large specialist retailing establishments (superstores) emerged to meet the needs of specific market segments.

More recently, developments with the World Wide Web have influenced the way of buying and shopping of goods and services. Many companies started using the Internet for cutting marketing costs, which results in reducing the cost of their items and services. It is also used by the companies to convey, transfer and disperse marketing information, to sell the product and to conduct customer surveys (Sinha, 2016). Customers use it as not only a means of purchasing the products online but also to compare various features of products offered by different stores and online retailers. In addition, shopping trips are being substituted with home deliveries.

How firms respond to environmental change

Firms can adopt a number of ways of coming to grips with the ever-changing complexity of the environment. Foremost among these is the implementation of an effective marketing information system (Buttery and Buttery, 1991) and the use of ongoing market research so that reaction time to change can be speeded up. Another approach involves what is called 'fast track' marketing. Increasing rates of technological change and the shortening of the life of products mean that companies have to act quickly when they are introducing new products to the market.

Late entrants to a market with a new product may find that the product does not offer attractive financial prospects, since the product's commercial life is much shorter than might have been typical some years ago. This is obviously most applicable to those industrial markets where product development times can be counted in years, for example military and commercial aircraft. The response is to look for ways of reducing the amount of time in developing and testing a product. The implication of this is that organizations have to 'manage in parallel' and not sequentially. This means that instead of one stage following on from another, wherever possible the two stages take place at the same time. Spending more money to speed up the process of innovation is another strategy, while spending more effort on planning things before something is put into action also appears to bear dividends.

Another area which is receiving considerable attention is preservation of the physical environment. Public awareness of the damage that processes and products can do the physical environment has increased the pressure on firms to act in a way which preserves the physical environment rather than destroys it. We explore ways in which firms are reacting to this challenge in the next section on 'green' marketing.

Green marketing

Green principles relate to the preservation of the environment. There are a number of issues which have important implications for marketing. These issues are now being tackled and, in many cases, firms take advantage of the fact that they are producing environmentally friendly products when they are promoting the products. The kinds of problems which exist and how firms are tackling these problems are discussed here.

Chemicals are a major force in environmental pollution. In an effort to make more productive use of land, intensive farming methods make use of artificial fertilizers and pesticides. Unfortunately, these can have a detrimental effect on the environment. The use of phosphates and bleaches in household detergents and the dumping of waste into rivers and the sea can also damage the environment. Packaging materials in which goods are shipped are a major contributor to waste. Over-packaging is being discouraged and the use of reusable or recyclable materials encouraged (Ginsberg and Bloom, 2004).

Legal environment and its influence on marketing activities

Sometimes, goods are bought that are not of merchantable quality, and it is not apparent at the time of purchase. The law exists to protect customers from unscrupulous manufacturers and dealers who produce shoddy, defective or dangerous goods. This also applies to the purchase of services.

Legislation may also be passed to curb unfair trading practices. This can occur when companies engage in trading practices which are not in the best interests of the customer. These include requirements with respect to the labelling and advertising of foods; the provision of remedies where goods or services purchased do not match with the descriptions given for them; and making it an offence for anyone to demand payment for goods or services that have not been ordered.

There are also acts concerning products offered at 'sale' prices; goods bought on credit; guarantees or conditions of sale; liability of traders for death or personal injury arising from negligence or from breach of duty; defects in products that give rise to damage; and the provision of a regulatory framework for the financial services industry. Legislation also covers anticompetitive practices in both public and private sectors.

Ethics and code of practice

Laws are enacted to deal with behaviour which is generally considered to be illegal. Defining the boundary between what might be considered lawful and what is not lawful can sometimes be a difficult task. For instance, something might not technically be considered illegal, yet it might be considered undesirable and even immoral. In this section we pay attention to actions which although not against the law may be considered to be undesirable and not in the best interests of the consumer.

In the setting of marketing, ethics relates to activities which although not actually illegal raise moral questions about their use. There are a range of other products that are more difficult to deal with since the products themselves are not illegal. Ethical issues also arise also in connection with how organizations market their products. Advertising which makes misleading claims about products or services and advertising which operates at a subliminal level are examples. Price fixing, although legally outlawed, may still operate since its existence may be difficult to substantiate. Moreover, distributors may fail to live up to agreements they have made with producers without the latter's knowledge.

Pressure groups, watchdogs and consumerism

The purpose of these groups is to influence how decisions that result in socially unacceptable consequences are made and to bring to the attention of the public and governments the need to outlaw such practices.

Watchdog organizations exist to deal with complaints about public sector organizations. Complaints received from users of these services are publicized. Another kind of group, environmental watchdog organizations, look out for matters relating to protecting the environment. They seek to oppose plans to build factories or houses in the open countryside in some cases and watch for environmental pollution caused by factories.

Consumerism is an organized movement established to guard the economic interests of consumers by compelling companies to behave in a socially responsible manner. Many organizations have produced voluntary codes of practice relating to matters which may give rise to environmental pollution as a result of pressure from consumerism (Trentmann, 2004).

Questions

1   What factors might give rise to inhospitable environments?
2   Why should some firms react only slowly to changing environments?
3   Discuss the various ways in which an organization can try to change its external environment.
4   How does society try to cope with deviant behaviour in the business environment? How does this affect what firms can and cannot do?
5   What kinds of ecological issues should organizations take into account when developing marketing strategies? Illustrate your answer with reference to real life examples.

References

Buttery, E. and Buttery, E. (1991), 'Design of a Marketing Information System: Useful Paradigms', *European Journal of Marketing*, 25(1): 26–39.

De Boef, S. and Kellstedt, P.M. (2004), 'The Political (and Economic) Origins of Consumer Confidence', *American Journal of Political Science*, 48(4): 633–649.

Ginsberg, J.M. and Bloom, P.N. (2004), 'Choosing the Right Green Marketing Strategy', *Sloan Management Review*, Fall: 79–84.

Sagiv, L. and Schwartz, S.H. (2007), 'Cultural Values in Organizations: Insights for Europe', *European Journal of International Management*, 1(3): 176–190.

Sinha, R. (2016), 'Investigating the Decision Making Style of College Student Regarding Online Apparel Shopping', *Journal of Exclusive Management Science*, 5(6): 639–647.

Trentmann, F. (2004), 'Beyond Consumerism: New Historical Perspectives on Consumption', *Journal of Contemporary History*, 39(3): 373–401.

Further reading

Camilleri, M.A. (2018), 'The Marketing Environment', in *Travel Marketing, Tourism Economics and the Airline Product*, Cham: Springer, pp. 51–68.

Carrier, J.G. (2019), *Ethical Consumption Social Value and Economic Practice*, New York, NY: Berghahn Books.

Gillespie, K. (2015), *Global Marketing*, 4th edition, New York: Routledge.

Jayasimha, K.R. and Billore, A. (2016), 'I Complain for Your Good? Re-Examining Consumer Advocacy', *Journal of Strategic Marketing*, 24(5): 360–376.

Lin, J., Lobo, A. and Leckie, C. (2019), 'The Influence of Green Brand Innovativeness and Value Perception on Brand Loyalty: The Moderating Role of Green Knowledge', *Journal of Strategic Marketing*, 27(1): 81–95.

Mason, R.B. (2007), 'The External Environment's Effect on Management and Strategy: A Complexity Theory Approach', *Management Decision*, 45(1): 10–28.

5   Customer and market analysis

Customer analysis

The marketing strategist needs to appreciate that consumers approach the purchase of different goods in different ways. The approaches taken have been thoroughly investigated, and a number of situations have been identified. Four main purchase situations are considered here:

- habitual purchases
- impulse buying
- limited decision making
- complex buying decisions

Habitual purchases

Frequently purchased items at the supermarket are often bought out of habit, and consumers do not undertake an extensive search for information nor do they engage in extensive evaluation prior to making a purchase. Consumers search for cues as to what the product is like. Colour of the packaging, for example, may be perceived by consumers to imply a given level of quality. The task of the marketing strategist has to discover the nature of these cues and ascertain the best way of making the product stand out on the shelves *vis-à-vis* competing products. In this sense, the products may then be seen to be 'putting themselves forward' to gain the attention of the consumer.

Repeated use of a product raises the confidence people have in using certain cues, and scanning becomes cursory in nature. Cues can stem from the product itself (intrinsic cues) – taste, texture, etc. – or can be produced by other attributes than the product (extrinsic cues) – brand name, packaging, advertising etc. People develop confidence in the reliability of certain cues and learn to choose with the help of extrinsic cues.

To make it easier to get to grips with their own understanding of several competing brands, consumers may categorize them according to several characteristics along a few dimensions. When confronted by a new brand, consumers will consider its likeness to each one of their mental categories and then judge its probable characteristics. In-store choice is predominantly based on the comparative assessment of rival brands.

Consumers purchase a particular brand because it is familiar, and the familiarity is accentuated by different types of advertising. The main job of marketers of competing brands is to persuade the consumer to switch brands. Trying out a new brand is the key, for then there is the possibility that the behaviour of repeatedly buying the same brand will be transferred to the new brand. Price and value for money are the principal factors which consumers consider in buying goods of this nature. Price and sales promotion are the key marketing variables for marketing strategists to use in such circumstances.

Impulse buying

Impulse buying for many people may well be the main method of purchasing, and it can create emotional friction in the mind of the consumer. This happens frequently where the price of goods is substantial relative to the purchaser's resources. The main task for the marketing strategist here is to allay cognitive dissonance. This may be achieved through advertising which is intended to specifically reassure purchasers that they have made a sensible choice in purchasing the product concerned.

Limited decision making

Consumers engage in this form of pre-purchase activity when they buy products only occasionally and when information is required regarding an unfamiliar brand. People spend a moderate amount of time gathering information and deliberating upon it prior to making a purchase. Marketing strategists need to pay attention to advertising that is informative in nature and which provides the potential purchasers with the kind of information they need to aid them in their decision making.

Complex buying decisions

Many people have studied consumer behaviour, and a five-stage model of the buying process has been distilled from these researches (see Engel et al., 1986). The implication is that consumers actually pass through all the stages in buying a product or service. In actual fact, of course, as we have seen in the case of habitual purchases, this is not necessarily the case. However, it is a useful framework from within which to view the purchase of many of the more expensive types of durable products and services. The stages are:

Recognizing that there is an unfulfilled want or need.
Searching for a way of satisfying the want or need.
Evaluating the options.
Buy or not buy.
Post-purchase behaviour – satisfaction or dissatisfaction.

It is suggested that marketers need to influence the consumers at each of these stages, including the last stage. Cognitive dissonance is often experienced by consumers after making a relatively expensive purchase. There is a tendency to ask oneself whether one has done the right thing in making the purchase or whether one would have been better off to have purchased a different brand, product or service altogether. Consumers need to be reassured. If the marketer has exaggerated the benefits of the product, then the consumer will more than likely experience dissatisfaction. This in turn can lead to poor word of mouth communication about the product to the consumer's circle of friends, relations and acquaintances.

Marketing people can do much to allay dissonance. Some of the methods include:

- Directing specific advertising at people who have already bought the product, featuring contented, happy customers.
- Writing booklets which are dissonance-reducing to accompany the product or service.
- Arranging speedy redress of customer grievances.

Formal models of consumer behaviour help firms to establish a framework within which to both understand behaviour and formulate communication strategies to take advantage of their understanding. However, one also needs to have an appreciation of the various factors that influence the consumer decision-making process. The major factors influencing consumer behaviour are marketing factors (promotion, distribution, price and the product specification), environmental factors, buyer characteristics and various people who may have been involved in the decision process. In the latter instance the following may have been influenced the decision outcome:

- user – user of the product or service,
- influencers – persons whose opinions may have been sought,

- deciders – those who actually have authority to take a decision,
- approver – whoever holds the purse strings,
- buyer – the person effecting the purchase and
- the person or thing which prevents the purchase being made.

Level of involvement

Highly priced goods that are visible to others often cause consumers to undertake considerable search for information before effecting a purchase. Such goods are known as high involvement goods. Clothing, furniture, cars and houses are products which fall readily into this category. Curiously, the degree of involvement for the same products may vary across people (Michaelidou and Dibb, 2008).

Postmodernism in consumer behaviour

One of the central themes of postmodernism relevant to marketing concerns consumer behaviour. In the 21st century, organizations operating in developed countries are supposedly dealing with well-educated and informed audiences. More to the point is that many consumers, irrespective of their level of educational attainment, are informed and well able to judge the merits of the variety of products and services and the advertising messages that accompany them. Moreover, in what today are comparatively affluent societies even by standards of 30 years ago, consumer choice has burgeoned and lessened the scope for market suppliers to dictate what consumers should buy. The consumers' main choice at the beginning of the 21st century is one of how to spend their money or wealth. Brand choice will always exist when consumers finally make up their minds how to spend their money, but it is persuading people to make up their minds in the first place that is now one of the predominant issues. Presented with a large variety of choices, consumers are beginning to question what they really want. In many cases, consumers may not really know what they want but only how to reject the unwanted alternatives. Indeed, it may be that consumers are not driven by needs but have needs which are driven by external forces (Firat, Dholakia and Venkatesh, 1995).

Organizational buying decisions

Organizational buyers are those purchasing goods and services for some tangibly productive and commercially meaningful purpose. They purchase on behalf of organizations operating across a wide spectrum of markets.

Primary concerns of organizational buyers

Delivery time is of paramount importance. Failure of a supplier to make promised deliveries can hold up production and cause considerable lost sales to a company. Reliability in terms of keeping to promised delivery dates is an important concern of organizational buyers because it can help to reduce the level of safety stocks kept and hence free-up working capital.

Specific services required vary in terms of importance. Market information, technical assistance, inventory maintenance, on-time delivery, repair service and credit facilities are commonly sought-after services.

Price influences operating costs and costs of goods sold. These in turn affect the customer's selling price and profit margin. When purchasing major equipment, for example, an industrial buyer looks upon the price as the amount of investment necessary to obtain a certain level of return or savings. This leads to a comparison of the price of a machine with the value of the benefits that the machine will yield.

Buying roles

Similarities with what we have outlined earlier in this chapter relating to roles in evaluating offerings exist. Firms marketing products should be aware of the various influential roles in decision making. Moreover, they need to identify the key influential people and to persuade them that the product will meet a felt need. (Webster and Wind, 1972)

Market analysis

Market analysis builds on customer and competitor analysis to allow strategic judgements to be made about a market and its dynamics. One of the primary objectives of a market analysis is to assess its prospects for participants. Another key purpose of market analysis is to understand the dynamics of the market. One needs to identify emerging key success factors, trends, threats and opportunities and to develop strategic questions that can guide information gathering and analysis.

Measuring the size of the market, identifying the trends and being able to predict how the market is going to develop in the future are critical factors in understanding the state of strategic windows.

A starting point is always the level of sales. Estimates of market size can be based on government sources or trade association findings. Another approach is to obtain information on competitors' sales from published financial sources, customers or even competitors. Still another, though more expensive, option is to survey customers and project their usage to the total market.

The potential market is also of interest. A new use, new user group or more frequent usage could change dramatically the size and prospects for the market. After the size of the market and its important sub-markets have been estimated, the focus turns to estimating trends in growth rates or decline rates. Often the most important strategic question involves the prediction of market sales and identifying the factors that will drive sales directly or indirectly.

Defining market demand

Demand can be measured at several levels:

* product levels – product item sales, product form sales, product line sales, company sales, industry sales, national sales;
* space levels – sales to individual customers, sales by territory, area or country, world sales; and
* time levels – short-range, medium-range, long-range sales.

There are 'penetrated markets', 'potential markets', 'available markets' and 'served markets'. The current number of users of a product or service and the sales volume they generate constitutes the 'penetrated market'. There may be figures readily available which indicate this, or it may be necessary to establish it by sample survey.

These estimates do not take account those people who have an interest in buying the product or service but who currently do not do so. The latter people are important because in looking at future demand they provide a measure of the 'potential market'. Customers must be able to afford the product or service, so in assessing the 'potential market' this must be established. This will redefine the market size.

Opportunity to use the product or service also cuts down on the size of the market. If it is not possible to use a product, then this will obviously restrict the market size. Taking this into account will define the 'available market'. A company has only a limited amount of resources at its disposal and so selects only certain market segments where it feels that it has the capacity to compete effectively and where the market size is sufficiently attractive. This becomes the 'served' or the 'target market'.

Predicting future demand

A company's production schedules, planned manning levels and financial budgeting are all related to the sales forecast. A too optimistic forecast can lead to excess stocks being accumulated, over-production and too high manning levels, and overborrowing or inefficient deployment of financial resources. A pessimistic forecast can lead to large opportunity costs and the creation of frustration among potential buyers of the company's products because delivery is late or not forthcoming.

Firms adopt a variety of approaches to sales forecasting, but the basic approach is to:

1   Make an environmental forecast regarding inflation, employment, interest rates, consumer spending and saving, business investment, etc.
2   Make a forecast of sales and profits to be earned by the industry using the data in stage 1 together with other information which links industry figures to environmental trends.
3   Make a company sales forecast using the data in stage 2 and assuming a given market share.

Often, however, firms may not know the industry sales level. In such cases sales forecasts are made at the company level at stage 2, and stage 3 is not used.

There are two basic approaches to forecasting sales for established products, both of which have a number of variants. On the one hand there are the methods which rely on asking people questions, and on the other hand there are those which involve the statistical or mathematical analysis of historical data.

Asking people questions

SURVEYS OF BUYERS' INTENTIONS

There are market research organizations which conduct periodic surveys of buying intentions. Using the results of regular sample surveys, predictions of the likely demand for various items are then prepared. Firms can of course carry out the surveys themselves, provided that they have the resources to do so. It is a method which can be applied effectively by producers of industrial plants, machinery and supplies.

COMPOSITE OF SALES FORCE OPINION

The sales force is in constant contact with the market and is in an excellent position to provide estimates on potential sales demand. When making use of estimates of the sales force one has to take into account any bias that may exist. For one reason or another the sales force may be biased either in the direction of pessimism or optimism. Another difficulty is that the sales force often may not really appreciate the larger economic factors which may influence sales. Providing one can identify sources of bias and adjust for them in interpreting predictions, it is possible to make use of these estimates.

EXPERT OPINION

Expert opinion is another method of forecasting. Experts may include dealers, distributors, suppliers, marketing consultants and even trade associations. A key factor which influences patterns of sales in a country is the state of its economy. Various economic experts can provide their opinions, and a government produces its own forecast for the economy.

Analyzing past data

Firms tend to base their forecasts on what they have achieved in the past. This approach to forecasting offers few opportunities for mistakes, except where there are large variations in sales from one year to the next.

Historical data can provide a useful perspective. However, the strategic interest is not on projections of history but rather on the prediction of turning points, which in turn requires lead indicators. Sales of related equipment or patterns of demographic data can often provide useful lead indicators. In both cases, of course, a reasonable lag between the change in the lead indicator and its impact on the sales of the firm or industry is required in order for it to be of use. Government forecasts of economic activity, provided experience shows them to be reasonably accurate, have a similar effect.

Market sales forecasts, especially of new markets, can be based on the experience of analogous industries. Of course, one has to be able to identify markets with similar characteristics.

Statistical demand analysis

Statistical demand analysis attempts to identify the source of all influences on demand so that more accurate forecasts can be made. The basic statistical method to take account of such factors is multiple regression analysis. Experience seems to indicate that the factors most commonly considered are price, income, population and marketing promotion.

The first stage in a regression analysis is to build a causal model in which one tries to explain sales in terms of a number of independent variables. For example, we might conjecture that industry sales of umbrellas are related to their relative price (P), personal disposable income (I), relative advertising expenditure and the absolute level of rainfall (*R*). We would express this relationship in the form of an equation:

$$S = a_0P + b_1I + b_2A + b_3R$$

What one has to do is to estimate the parameters for $a_0, b_1 \ldots b_3$ and apply them to quantifications of *P*, *I*, *A* and *R* for the period of the forecast.

In principle, demand equations of this variety are acquired by fitting the best equations to historical or cross-sectional data. The coefficients of the equation are estimated according to what is called the 'least squares criterion'. According to this criterion, the best equation is the one that minimizes a measure of the error between the actual and the predicted observation.

Forecasting sales of new products

To forecast sales of new products, one needs some initial sales figures with which to work. Given that early sales data are available, it is then generally possible by using one or other of a variety of mathematical models or 'curve fitting routines' to make some prediction for sales over a specified period of time. Alternatively, it may be possible to look at sales histories of similar new products and make predictions by analogy. There are numerous examples of these models.

Large retail chains often add new lines to their stock. Most of these retailers have benchmarks against which to judge whether a product is likely to be successful or not. A common practice is to offer the product for sale for a limited period in one of its shops. If the product fails to achieve a certain level of sales within the specified period, it is withdrawn from sale and not put on sale in other outlets.

Long-term forecasting

The overall process starts with a simple form of scenario forecasting. The techniques have been derived from those traditionally used, most notably from those publicized by Shell (Van Der Heijden, 1996). Whatever approach is adopted, this is the most complex part of the overall planning process. On the other hand, the simpler it is, the better it works, not least because those involved understand what is happening. One focuses on the key 'drivers' for change – things that affect the industry being investigated, over a two-decade time scale – without exploring the complications. As a result, we may lose some 'accuracy', especially in terms of the fine detail about the future the process reveals. On the other hand, we are able to detect almost all the key developments, certainly all those which have surfaced by other methods, covering the great majority of expected 'drivers'. This part of the overall planning process can be undertaken in as little time as half a day. It might involve a management team of six to eight members, using a variation on well-understood focus group techniques combined with some from scenario forecasting – and with little more than Post-it notes stuck on a wall to facilitate their thinking. Even so, this is a critical aspect of the process, since only if the key turning points are identified in these scenarios will the (robust) strategies developed in response be valid.

Questions

1 One of the primary objectives of a market analysis is to assess its prospects for participants. Another key purpose of market analysis is to understand the dynamics of the market. Indicate how these objectives might be achieved.

2 Many consumer-purchasing situations involve complex buying decisions. Describe some situations which illustrate this point and explain how the 'five stages in the buying process' model is relevant to these situations.

3 'The goods and services people buy represent an extension of their own personalities'. Discuss.

4 How does postmodernism impact on marketing activities in the 21st century?

5 Suggest how a company might forecast company sales for the following products:

    a   current pharmaceutical medicines supplied to be supplied to hospitals and pharmacists.

    b   yearly sales of agricultural tractors.

    c   long range sales of existing commercial aircraft.

    d   a range of fashion clothes in a chain of boutique outlets.

    e   online monthly sales of a vast range of non-food items.

    f   daily sales of fish at a supermarket.

References

Engel, J.F., Blackwell, R.D. and Miniard, P.W. (1986), *Consumer Behaviour*, 5th edition, New York: Holt, Rinehart & Winston.

Firat, A.F., Dholakia, N. and Venkatesh, A. (1995), 'Marketing in a Postmodern World', *European Journal of Marketing*, 29(1): 40–56.

Michaelidou, N. and Dibb, S. (2008), 'Consumer Involvement: A New Perspective', *Marketing Review*, 8(1): 83–99.

Van Der Heijden, K. (1996), *Scenarios: The Art of Strategic Conversation*, Chichester: John Wiley.

Webster, F.E. and Wind, Y. (1972), 'A General Model for Understanding Organizational Buying Behavior', *Journal of Marketing*, 36(2): 12–19.

Further reading

Brown, S. and Turley, D. (eds.). (1997), *Consumer Research*, London: Routledge.
Chaney, D., Touzani, M. and Slimane, K.B. (2017), 'Marketing to the (New) Generations: Summary and Perspectives', *Journal of Strategic Marketing*, 25(3): 179–189.
Hansen, F. and Hansen, M.M. (2005), 'Children as Innovators and Opinion Leaders', *Young Consumers*, 6(2): 44–59.
Lim, W.M. (2017), 'Untangling the Relationships between Consumer Characteristics, Shopping Values, and Behavioral Intention in Online Group Buying', *Journal of Strategic Marketing*, 25(7): 547–566.
Parsons, E., MacLaran, P. and Chatzidakis, A. (2016), *Contemporary Issues in Marketing and Consumer Behavior*, 2nd edition, Oxford: Taylor and Francis.
Pozza, I.D., Heitz-Spahn, S. and Texier, L. (2017), 'Generation Y Multichannel Behaviour for Complex Services: The Need for Human Contact Embodied through a Distance Relationship', *Journal of Strategic Marketing*, 25(3): 226–239.

6 Sustainable competitive advantage

Competitive advantage is achieved through the positioning of one firm's offering relative to another. An alternative view suggests that it is superior resources and processes designed to utilize such resources efficiently that will create a competitive advantage. Both approaches are not mutually exclusive and can be complementary. Indeed, such a view is in keeping with the view of keeping open the strategic window of opportunity.

Core competencies

Core competencies are a combination of technological and managerial capabilities which provide the firm with a leadership position in the development of certain generic or core products. They may relate to world leadership in specific technologies, or they may be related to particular organizational or managerial skills. Core competencies apply also in the services sector, though in this case the competencies may be related to technology imported from manufacturing. For example, fast cycle times are a critical factor in providing customer service in many industries.

Core competencies and competitive advantage

Through the identification of its distinctive competencies and the relating of them to its core products, a firm can develop strategies and plans which make best use of those capabilities. New capabilities might then be sought after in order to achieve greater sustainable advantage.

In searching for a competitive advantage, businesses often develop capabilities in key functional areas (Prahalad and Hamel, 1990). To be sustainable, these capabilities must be difficult to imitate and should support the organization's business strategy (Day, 1994).

The development of key marketing capabilities has been identified as one of the primary ways firms can achieve a competitive advantage (Day,

1990, 1994). In this context, firms must develop processes that allow them to collect information about market opportunities, develop goods and services to meet the needs of targeted customers in selected markets, price these products according to market information, communicate product advantages to potential customers and distribute products to customers (Day, 1994).

Organizational capabilities assist in the process of achieving a competitive advantage.

Generic strategies

Porter (1985) suggested the alternatives of a low-cost strategy, a differentiation strategy and a focused strategy. The low-cost strategy involves the sacrifice of some quality, fashion and even product innovation in order to keep costs low – the lowest in the industry. With this strategy there is also an assumption that the achievement of production economies of scale is a significant factor in success. This contrasts with a differentiation strategy, which focuses on the factors ignored by the low-cost strategy such as product variety, quality and service, but again implicit is the notion that size matters to achieve successful differentiation. Smaller firms are advised to move towards strategies which target small subsegments of the market to avoid competition with larger businesses for whom these segments are too small and specialized to be of interest.

Low-cost strategies

Although there is a tendency to think of low-cost strategies as a single approach such as scale economies, low-cost labour or production automation, there are many methods of obtaining a low-cost advantage. The successful low-cost firms are those that can harness multiple approaches.

No frills product/service: A direct approach to low cost is to remove all frills and extras from a product or service. A major risk, especially in the service sector, is that competitors will add just a few features and position themselves against a no-frills firm. The goal is to generate a cost advantage that is sustainable for one of two reasons. First, competitors cannot easily stop offering services that their customers expect. Second, competitors' operations and facilities have been designed for such services and cannot easily be changed. A firm with an inherent cost advantage has a good chance of success with a no-frills approach.

Product design: A product's design or composition can create cost advantages. A variant is to augment a product with relatively high-margin accessories or extra features and thus provide a higher perceived value to customers. Product downsizing is another approach that can be helpful when price pressures inhibit alternatives.

Differentiation

A differentiation strategy is one in which a product offering is different from that of one or more competitors in a way that is valued by the customers. The value added should affect customer choice and ultimate satisfaction. Ways of differentiating by adding value include being able to do something better than competitors or providing an extra product feature or service.

There are many approaches or strategic orientations that can lead to sustainable differentiation strategies. These include the use of strategic information systems, global thinking, being innovative, being customer driven or employing a unique distribution system. Employing quality and building strong brands, however, are two of the most important approaches.

The quality option: A quality strategy involves delivering and being perceived to deliver a product or service superior to that of competitors. A quality strategy can mean that the brand will be a premium brand as opposed to a value or economy entry.

To be the quality option, a business must distinguish itself with respect to delivering quality to customers. What is required is a quality-focused management system that is comprehensive, integrative and supported throughout the organization.

The quality option is designed ultimately to improve customer satisfaction. It follows that a customer focus will be part of a successful effort. One indicator of a customer focus is the involvement of top management. A hallmark of most customer-driven organizations is that the top executives have regular meaningful one-to-one contact with customers. Another indicator is the link to the compensation and measurement system. It is crucial to understand not only what is important with respect to quality but also what drives those quality perceptions.

Building strong brands

Differentiation can also be accomplished by building strong brands to create brand equity (Keller, 2009). This strategy is likely to prove sustainable since it creates competitive barriers. Brand equity generates value to the customer that can emerge either as a price premium or enhanced brand loyalty. Brand equity is a set of assets and liabilities linked to a brand's name and symbol that add to or subtract from the value provided by a product or service to a firm or that firm's customers. The assets and liabilities on which brand equity is based differ according to the situation. They are:

1 *Brand awareness*
   This gives the product or service a sense of familiarity. In the case of low involvement products this familiarity can be an important influence in the purchase decision.
2 *Brand identity*
   A brand identity reflects the associations attached to a firm and its brands. These associations are usually those of product attributes or customer benefits. A brand's associations are assets that can create confidence and trust, affect feelings towards a product and provide the basis for brand extensions. They can provide an important basis for differentiation where it is difficult to distinguish objectively between various brands.
3 *Brand loyalty*
   Brand loyalty or resistance to switching can be based on lack of motivation to change from the existing brand, a genuine liking for an existing brand or the actual cost of switching. Switching costs reflect the sunk investment that has to be sacrificed in order to switch from one brand to another. Switching costs will be lower for fast-moving consumer goods but clearly higher for durable consumer white goods. An existing base of loyal customers provides an enormous sustainable competitive advantage. It reduces the marketing costs of doing business since existing customers are relatively easy to hold whereas getting and retaining new ones is more difficult.

   The loyalty of existing customers represents a substantial industry/ market entry barrier to would-be competitors. Excessive resources are required when entering a market in which existing customers must be cajoled away from an established brand with which they are well satisfied. The profit potential for the tentative entrant is thus reduced.

Brands and strategy

Branding for consumers represents the mark of a given level of quality and value that helps them choose between one offering and another. The development of a range of brands to cover different consumer segments enables a firm to benefit from changing consumer wants. From a marketer's point of view, brands allow the producer, and more recently the retailer, to target different groups of consumers or segments of the market with different label product offerings. In fact, developing more than one brand enables a firm to segment a market and target different consumers. The development of a portfolio of discrete brands enables a firm to isolate the problems of one product from the rest of the range, and it can enable it to divest less profitable brands.

Brand trends at the retail level

The preparedness of branded goods producers to supply own label products for retailers stems partly from a need to take up spare production capacity, but it is also indicative of the need to prevent complete erosion of the existing sales base. The willingness of leading producers to supply own label products has also reduced the quality gap between own labels and producer brands.

The sophistication of retailers' own marketing communications, particularly packaging and promotion styles, has strengthened their credibility in terms of ability to deliver satisfying products. Retailers have used advertising to create a brand image which has been reinforced by unique design features applied to store layouts, staff training and their own label product ranges. Retailers often develop differentiated ranges of own label products to meet segmented customer needs.

Seen from the point of view of producers, it can be argued that the power of the buyer (the retailer) has been strengthened by the product-market strategies which the retailers pursue. Own brands do not meet the formal definition of substitute products, but they certainly perform the function of such products.

Counter strategies available to producers

Producers use database and direct marketing to try to get closer to the consumer. Producers also meet the new challenge from own label brands by investing in the development of innovative products which can be shown to have demonstrably different advantages over own label products. Producers are also able to take advantage of their more focused image – since retailers supply such a wide range of products – and producers may very well benefit from developing products in partnership with one another.

Producer retailer partnerships

Problems created by the emergence of own brands may be circumvented by producers and retailers getting together and co-operating. Partnerships where both sides are working for mutual advantage seem to be fruitful avenues for exploration. The extent to which a producer can obtain cooperation from a retailer does depend upon how much value the latter places on its supplier's marketing and product development expertise. In general, retailers are in the more powerful position since they have gained leverage in the retailer–producer bargaining interface. Faced with the increasing power of retailers, producers need to gain and take notice of the needs and views of retailers.

There is a need for joint product development projects and joint marketing ventures between producers and retailers. Moreover, producers can augment their product offerings with product add-ons, including services to retailers and consumers with respect to delivery, after-sales contact, financing and promotion. A producer's strength will be defined not just in terms of the brand strength but in terms of the skills of staff assigned to managing brands, retailers and consumers and the flexibility and effectiveness of the organization structure within which they operate.

Ethical branding

Ethics are a potentially powerful influence on consumer decisions. There are certainly many consumers who would prefer to choose ethically safe products and companies. It is reflective of a deep shift in public expectations of what brands do and what they stand for. Increasing marketing literacy, the rise of pressure groups and the development of the consumer press are making people realize that ethical issues are deeply embedded in society. Moreover, relative prosperity in developed countries is affording the consumers in these countries the luxury of worrying about these things and the opportunity to express their approval or disapproval in how they spend their money.

Brands have to take an ethical stance in ethical matters when it relates to matters which impact on the environment. The key issue is judging the acceptable price that consumers are willing to pay for adhering to their ethical principles. Consumers are price conscious, though the existence of an affluent society can shift the upper boundary to their discretionary purchasing activity and hence allow some degree of ethical consideration to enter into their purchasing decisions.

Focus strategies

The focus strategic thrust, whether it involves differentiation, low cost or both, concentrates on one part of the market or product line. A focus strategy avoids strategy dilution or distraction and is more likely to lead to competitive advantage. When the internal investment programmers and culture have all been directed towards a single end and there is buy-in on the part of everyone in the organization, the result will be assets, skills and functional strategies that match market needs. In most cases the product line or market is expanded and compromises are made in advertising, distribution, manufacturing and so on. Moreover, the strategic competitive advantage and associated entry barriers will be diluted.

A business that lacks the resources to compete in a broad product market must focus in order to generate the impact that is needed to compete effectively. A focus strategy provides the potential to bypass competitor assets and skills. It can also provide a positioning device. Although pay-off of a small niche may be less than that of a growing market, the competition may often also be less intense. Large growth markets attract many competitors and stimulate overcapacity, whereas this is unlikely to occur in niche markets to the same extent.

Nevertheless, a focus strategy does limit the potentials of a business. Profitable sales may well be missed, and the business may have to compete with firms that enjoy scale economies. Moreover, a multi-focus strategy may be better than a single focus one. (Tallon, 2007)

Focusing the product line

Focusing on part of a product line can enhance the line's technical superiority. In most businesses, the key people have expertise or interest in a few products. As the product line broadens, however, the products tend to be 'me too' products which do not provide value and detract from the base business. This may spur on the need to remain focused and resist product expansion.

Targeting a segment

The same argument applies as in focusing the product line.

Low-share competitors

In many industries there is a dominant firm with substantial scale advantages. A key to competing against such firms is usually to use some variant of focus strategy. One approach is to look for a portion of the market in which the dominant firm is making high profits which may be used to subsidize other parts of its business. Another is to focus on a part of the market that has been neglected and develop an offering and strategy to capture it.

The pre-emptive move

This is the implementation of a strategy new to a business area that, because it is first, generates a skill or asset that competitors are inhibited or prevented from duplicating or countering. A sustainable first-mover advantage can result from technological leadership, pre-emption of assets and/or buyer switching costs. Pre-emptive moves can be directed at supply systems, products, production systems, customers or distribution and service systems.

A business can gain advantage by pre-empting access to the best or least expensive sources of raw materials or production equipment. Like many pre-emptive moves, those oriented toward the supply system are risky. If supply commitments are made and business does not materialize or other superior supply sources emerge, such a strategy could backfire.

The first product to be introduced in a market can enjoy the substantial advantage of occupying a desirable position. It allows the first entrant the opportunity to adopt whatever positioning strategy it wants. A new competitor is almost forced into another positioning strategy. A key in some industries is to become the industry standard. A first mover can develop customer loyalty by creating switching costs.

Questions

1   How are core competencies related to strategy formulation?
2   How relevant are Porter's generic strategy typologies in the 21st century?
3   Given the increasing power of retailers in consumer goods marketing, how has this affected producers' brand strategy?
4   How might ethical branding issues be featured in the way in which organizations promote and otherwise market themselves?
5   Are focus strategies becoming more important? Why or why not?

References

Day, G.S. (1990), *Market Driven Strategy, Processes for Creating Value*, New York: The Free Press.

Day, G.S. (1994), 'The Capability of Market Driven Organizations', *Journal of Marketing*, 58(3): 37–52.

Keller, K.L. (2009), 'Building Strong Brands in a Modern Marketing Communications Environment', *Journal of Marketing Communications*, 15(2–3): 139–155.

Porter, M.E. (1985), *Competitive Advantage*, New York: The Free Press.

Prahalad, C.K. and Hamel, G. (1990), 'The Core Competence of the Corporation', *Harvard Business Review*, 68(3): 79–91.

Tallon, P.P. (2007), 'Does IT Pay to Focus? An Analysis of IT Business Value under Single and Multi-Focused Business Strategies', *The Journal of Strategic Information Systems*, 16(3): 278–300.

Further reading

Brooksbank, R. and Taylor, D. (2007), 'Strategic Marketing in Action: A Comparison of Higher and Lower Performing Manufacturing Firms in the UK', *Marketing Intelligence and Planning*, 25(1): 31–44.

Davcik, N.S. and Sharma, P. (2016), 'Marketing Resources, Performance, and Competitive Advantage: A Review and Future Research Directions', *Journal of Business Research*, 69(12): 5547–5552.

Denrell, J. and Powell, T.C. (2016), 'Dynamic Capability as a Theory of Competitive Advantage: Contributions and Scope Conditions', in D.J. Teece and S. Heaton (eds.), *The Oxford Handbook of Dynamic Capabilities*, Oxford: Oxford University Press.

Hakkak, M. and Ghodsi, M. (2015), 'Development of a Sustainable Competitive Advantage Model Based on Balanced Scorecard', *International Journal of Asian Social Science*, 5(5): 298–308.

Srivastava, R.K. and Fahey, L. and Christensen, H.K. (2001), 'The Resource-Based View and Marketing: The Role of Market-Based Assets in Gaining Competitive Advantage', *Journal of Management*, 27(6): 777–802.

Tsougkou, E., Cadogan, J.W., Hodgkinson, I.R., Oliveira, J.S., Abdul-Talib, A.N., Story, V.M. and Lioliou, E. (2019), 'Achieving Export Competitive Advantage: Can Global Orientation and Export Product Adaptation Be Reconciled?', Paper presented at 2019 AMA Global Marketing SIG Conference, Buenos Aires, Argentina.

7　Growth strategies

Growth strategies

Ansoff's (1957) product-market expansion grid provides a useful though not exhaustive framework for looking at possible strategies to cope with the problem of strategic windows and finding ways of creating overlapping strategic windows. He identified four generic strategies: market penetration, product development, market development and diversification. The concept of the product-market expansion grid is shown in Figure 7.1.

Generic strategies based on the product-market expansion grid are:

ANSOFF MATRIX – GENERIC STRATEGIES

Market Penetration Strategy	*Product Development Strategy*
Increase purchase use by existing customers	New features
Win customers from competition	Different quality levels
Convert non-users	New products
Market Development Strategy	*Diversification Strategy*
New market segments	Through organic growth
New distribution channels	Through acquisition
New geographic markets	Through joint venture

Market penetration strategy of existing markets

Here the strategy amounts to increasing sales of existing products while at the same time trying to maintain current margins of profitability on sales. When the market is expanding this may be accomplished with nominal outlays of marketing expenditure by getting more first-time users to buy the product, to increase product usage of existing buyers or to increase the frequency of use. In a saturated market, extra sales may only be generated

	Existing products	New products
Existing Markets	Market penetration strategy	Product development strategy
New Markets	Market development strategy	Diversification strategy

Figure 7.1 The product-market expansion grid

as a result of increased market share. Another possibility, however, is to promote new applications for existing product users. Such new uses can best be identified by market research aimed at determining exactly how customers use the brand.

Increasing market share puts heavy pressure on marketing resources and can impact negatively on short-run profitability. However, if economies of scale or the impact of the 'experience curve' are felt as a result of increased supply to the market, then this may more than offset the impact on profitability of any additional marketing expenditure.

A share gain can be based on tactical actions such as advertising, trade allowances, promotions or price reductions. The problem is that such share gains can be difficult to sustain. A preferred option is to generate a more permanent share gain by winning a sustainable competitive advantage with enhanced customer value or by matching a competitor's sustainable competitive advantage. The aim is to create or enhance the assets and skills of the business and neutralize those of competitors.

Attempts to increase market share will very likely affect competitors directly and therefore precipitate competitor responses. The alternative of attempting to increase usage among current customers is usually less threatening to competitors. Heavy users are usually the most fruitful target. Light users, however, should not be ignored because there may be a way to unlock their potential. Increased product usage can in fact be stimulated in three different ways. First, the frequency can be increased. Second, the quantity used in each application can be increased. And finally, new applications can be promoted.

In order to increase the frequency of use, reminder communications are necessary. In the case of getting people to use more of the product, this may simply involve repositioning the product from one which is used occasionally to one that is used regularly, and this can be achieved through a repositioning promotional campaign. Other increases of frequency of purchase may be sought through providing incentives – competitions and sales promotions.

Similar techniques can be used to increase the quantity used on each occasion, that is, reminder communications and incentives.

Product development strategy

The introduction of new products can have a positive impact on sales growth. Initially, profitability may not increase, since there may be substantial research, development and launching costs associated with the venture which have to be recouped. A 'new product' can be defined in several different ways. A product can refer to a physical entity or a cluster of expected customer benefits, depending on whether the perspective adopted is that of the business or that of the market. From the point of view of a business, a product innovation may represent a change in or addition to the physical entities that make up its product line. From a market perspective, the term refers to a new or revised set of customer perceptions about a particular cluster of benefits. Thus, that which is considered a product innovation by a business enterprise may not be recognized as such by its customers. Here we will adopt a business perspective.

A new product is one that is new in any way for the company concerned (McCarthy and Perreault, 1993). Additions to existing product lines and improvements of an existing product may also be thought of as 'new products'. In practice only a few new products are actually new to the firm and new to the market.

New product failures

Innovation may be thought of as the cornerstone of success in many industries, but not all innovations are successful. Indeed, the incidence of failure in introducing new products is substantially high (Crawford, 1987). Of course, what is a failure for one firm may well be a successful product for another firm. It all depends upon the expectations of the firm. Failures are never absolute entities in themselves. The usual measure taken when evaluating the comparative success of a new product is the financial return on investment it generates. But of course, what will satisfy one company will not necessarily satisfy another.

A methodical approach to screening new and developing new products

There are a variety of ways of obtaining new product ideas: monitoring competitors' new product development, feedback from customers, market research, contact with R&D establishments and a firm's own R&D. There is not one best method, and firms should try all methods wherever possible (Soukhoroukova et al., 2012).

Screening

The likely financial performance and implications of developing and/or adopting a new product idea are the key factors that need to be taken into account. However, without undertaking desk and/or field research it is difficult to quantify what we might expect to sell. Pooled estimates of subjective expert opinions, however, can sometimes provide remarkably close estimates. Members of the firm who might have some idea of the quantities of the various new product ideas that the firm might expect to sell should be consulted. With such estimates it should then be possible to make rough financial estimates of likely profits to be generated. These rough estimates are turned into more precise estimates at the third phase – business analysis – where a full quantitative analysis and evaluation is made. The initial screening stage is characterized by a checklist of benchmarks which new products have to satisfy before they can be moved on to the next phase in the six-step process.

For example:

- Is the product compatible with present distribution channels?
- Is the product complementary to current products?
- Can it be priced competitively alongside products of a similar quality?
- Will promotion of the product be easy?
- Will there always be uses for the product?
- Is there a wide variety of potential customers?
- Are existing resources sufficient to facilitate production and marketing of the product?
- Will the product fill an unsatisfied need in the marketplace?
- Is the market likely to grow in size?

Experience seems to indicate that successful products:

- fit well with the internal functional strengths of the business and
- fit with the need of the market.

Business analysis

At the business analysis phase, sales, costs and profit projections have to be made in order to determine whether the adoption of the new product into the product mix will satisfy company objectives. The phase involves predicting sales and cost behaviour so that profitability of the product can be estimated. This can be done in a variety of ways, and it is always advisable to use as many different ways as is feasible. Approaches include:

- examining sales histories of similar products,
- surveying market opinion,
- using expert opinions and
- statistical models.

Irrespective of the approach taken, minimum and maximum sales estimates need to be obtained to provide an idea of the amount of risk involved. The method of forecasting depends on whether the product is a one-time purchase, an infrequently purchased product or a frequently purchased product. In the case of infrequently purchased products, attention has to be given to predicting first-time sales and replacement sales. In the case of frequently purchased products, attention has to be given to first-time buyers and repeat purchases. In using any of the identified methods of forecasting it is essential to gain a separate estimate, as appropriate, of

- first-time purchase,
- replacement purchase and
- repeat purchase.

Costs also have to be estimated, and these may change over the time span of the sales forecast. This has to be taken into account when estimating profits and likely sales because costs do have uncertainties attached to them. Escalating prices of raw materials or bought-in parts can stifle the sales growth of a new product because of the need to continually adjust its price upwards.

Placing a value on the financial appeal of a new product is of course very important. However, it does have to be borne in mind that a large amount of uncertainty surrounds any estimates that are made. Moreover, there is always the danger that once numbers are put down on paper they will be treated as if they represent certainties. It is therefore a good idea to keep in mind the more qualitative aspects of evaluation, as defined in the checklist of criteria used at the screening stage.

Surveys of market opinion can be particularly helpful at the business analysis phase since in addition to helping to quantify potential demand they can also help to provide other information as well. It may be possible that with some adjustment to the product or service it will sell better. It is important to get this right at the outset. The kind of qualitative questions to ask here relate to whether:

- the benefits of using the product are clear to the user,
- the product solves a problem or fills a need,
- other products already fill this need and give satisfaction or
- the price is right in relationship to the perceived value.

One should, of course, pick an appropriate group of target customers. Where the new product is only a concept it can be presented symbolically. At this stage a word and/or a picture description will suffice. Products that satisfy the criteria set for this phase can then move on to the product development phase, where the feasibility of creating a satisfactory product can be tested. Subsequent to this the product may be test marketed with consumers to gauge their reactions.

Test marketing

Where launch costs are high it would seem commonsense to test market new products before embarking on commercialization on a national or international scale. However, not all products are test marketed. It is possible under certain circumstances that test marketing the product may provide important business knowledge to competitors. Nevertheless, test marketing, on the other hand, can avoid disasters and save firms millions of pounds.

The amount of test marketing to be given to a product reflects investment cost and risk on the one hand and pressure of time and cost of research on the other. Clearly the greater the amount of investment, the more need there is to proceed with thorough testing. The same is also true of high-risk new products.

Market development strategy

Finding new markets does not guarantee long-term or short-term profitability, but economies of scale in producing for the market or in supplying the market will contribute to profitability. However, there may well be barriers to entry to the market, which means that neither short-run nor long-term contributions to overall profitability are attractive.

A logical avenue of growth is to develop new markets by duplicating the business operation, perhaps with minor adaptive changes. In the case of market expansion, the same expertise and technology and sometimes even the same plant and operations facility can be used. There is thus potential synergy and resulting reductions in investment and operating costs. Of course, market development is based upon the premise that the business is operating successfully.

Geographic expansion may involve changing from a regional operation to a national operation, moving into another region, or expanding to another country. A firm can also grow by reaching into new market segments. There is, of course, a variety of ways to define target segments and hence growth directions. A key to detecting new markets is to consider a wide variety of segmentation variables. Sometimes looking at a market from different perspectives will uncover useful segments:

- usage – the non-user can be an attractive target;
- distribution system – new markets can be reached by opening up additional distribution channels; and
- age – pulling in additional age categories in the population (consumer goods).

Diversification

Diversification involves moving simultaneously into new products and new markets. It is a risky strategy, but with careful selection of the right kind of businesses, considerable improvements in profitability can be experienced. Diversification represents an opportunity for growth and revitalization. A diversification strategy can be implemented by an acquisition (or merger), new business venture or strategic alliance.

Moving into areas where a firm does not have any prior experience is highly risky, and firms may prefer to move into related markets. Moreover, there may be some synergy to be gained from moving into related markets. The synergy may be in marketing or even in production. In theory, as a result of diversification, the business should be able to improve its return on investment (ROI) because of increased revenues, decreased costs or reduced investment. Meaningful commonalties can involve similar

- distribution channels,
- images and their impact on the market,

- sales and advertising efforts,
- facilities,
- production processes,
- R&D efforts,
- operating systems and
- staff needs.

It is important to determine whether there is any real area of commonality that will affect the ROI. Sometimes an unrelated diversification can be justified, but it does require a different rationale. Indeed, firms need to consider whether any form of diversification is the best strategy in a given situation (Hoskisson and Hitt, 1990).

Vertical integration

Vertical integration can take two forms. It can be forward integration, as when a producer takes over a distributor, or backward integration, as is the case when a manufacturer takes over a supplier. Integrative strategies enable firms to gain greater control over the chain of production and distribution. For example, a manufacturer may have difficulty in gaining vital components from a supplier. It may be because the supplier is also selling the same component to other firms and cannot produce enough to satisfy everyone. Under such circumstances the manufacturer may be tempted to try to buy out the supplier (i.e. become the owner of the supplier's business) to ensure that it can always have supplies of the key component.

A good way to understand when vertical integration should be considered and how it should be evaluated is to look at the possible benefits and costs of a vertical integration strategy. These may be such things as:

> *Benefits – operating economies, access to supply or demand, control of the product system, entry into a profitable business, enhanced technological innovation.*

Combining operations can result in improved production and related economies. In some contexts, a key success factor is access to a supply of raw material, a part or another input factor – backward integration can reduce the risk. Similarly, forward integration could be motivated by concern about product outlets. Whenever only one buyer and one seller exist for highly specialized products and services, there will be an incentive to consider vertical integration. When such specialization occurs, there is a real danger that one party may hold up the other by taking opportunistic advantage of a change in either its circumstance or the environment. It may be necessary to integrate vertically to gain sufficient control over a product or service to maintain the integrity of a differentiation strategy. Vertical integration may be the only way to ensure that quality is maintained. A vertical integration decision can be motivated by an attractive profit potential or an advantage in achieving technological innovation.

Costs – operating costs, management of a different business, increase in risk, reduced flexibility, cost of inward focus.

Vertical integration often involves adding an operation that requires organizational assets and skills which differ markedly from those of a firm's other business areas. As a result, the firm may not be suited to run the integrated operation effectively and competitively. The classic way to reduce risk is to avoid having too many eggs in one basket – to diversify. Vertical integration tends to increase the amount of commitment and investment that are tied to a certain market. If that market is healthy, then integration may enhance profits. On the other hand, if the market turns down, integration may cause profits to be more depressed. Integration also raises exit barriers. If the business becomes weak, the additional investment and commitment created by integration will inhibit consideration of an exit alternative. Furthermore, if one operation becomes dependent on the other, it may be awkward to try to exit from one.

Vertical integration usually means that a firm is committed to an in-house supplier or customer. The flexibility of changing suppliers may be limited because of commitment made to an integration partner. There is often a trade-off between flexibility and commitment. Increased commitment provides the potential of higher profits but is associated with a reduction in the ability to adapt to changing circumstances (Balakrishnan and Wernerfelt, 1986).

Evaluating growth strategies

A similar kind of evaluation to that used with regards to product development should be applied to market development and diversification strategies. Evaluating vertical integration strategies would be more complex. Generally, effect on cash flow is a major concern when examining alternative courses of action. One needs to treat each alternative as a project and estimate the nature of anticipated cash flows over the period of time that the project is likely to be alive. Initial and end of project flows have to be taken into account as well inflows and outflows of cash during the time the project is up and running. Initial investment and one-time set up costs may be needed at the beginning, while there may be disposal costs and shut down costs at the end of the project and even inflows of cash resulting from selling equipment at scrap or residual values.

Questions

1   How might the Ansoff matrix be usefully employed when looking for new marketing strategies?
2   In what order should an organization consider the various strategic approaches which make up the Ansoff matrix along with integrative strategies? In particular, when is each one most appropriate?
3   What is a new product? What is a new product success? How can risk of failure in introducing products to the market be minimized?
4   Diversification is simply a form of horizontal integration. To what extent would you agree with this point of view?
5   What are the benefits and disadvantages of vertical integration? How might the advantages best be sought in the 21st century?

References

Ansoff, H.I. (1957), 'Strategies for Diversification', *Harvard Business Review*, 35(5): 113–124.
Balakrishnan, S. and Wernerfelt, B. (1986), 'Technical Change, Competition and Vertical Integration', *Strategic Management Journal*, 7(4): 347–350.
Crawford, C.M. (1987), 'New Product Failure Rates: A Reprise', *Research Management*, 30(4): 20–24.
Hoskisson, R. and Hitt, M. (1990), 'Antecedents and Performance Outcomes of Diversification: A Review and Critique of Theoretical Perspectives', *Journal of Management*, 16(2): 461–509.
McCarthy, E.J. and Perreault, W.D. (1993), *Basic Marketing*, 11th edition, Chicago, IL: Richard D. Irwin, p. 299.
Soukhoroukova, A., Spann, M. and Skiera, B. (2012), 'Sourcing, Filtering, and Evaluating New Product Ideas: An Empirical Exploration of the Performance of Idea Markets', *Journal of Product Innovation Management*, 29(1): 100–112.

Further reading

Daneels, E. (2002), 'The Dynamics of Product Innovation and Firm Competences', *Strategic Management Journal*, 23(12): 1095–1121.

Hult, G.T., Hurley, R. and Knight, G. (2004), 'Innovativeness: Its Antecedents and Impact on Business Performance', *Industrial Marketing Management*, 33(5): 429–438.

Kahn, K.B. (2002), 'An Exploratory Investigation of New Product Forecasting Practices', *Journal of Product Innovation Management*, 19(2): 133–143.

Ulwick, A.W. (2002), 'Turn Customer Input into Innovation', *Harvard Business Review*, 80(1): 91–97.

8 Segmentation, targeting and positioning

Segmentation

Market segmentation is essential in the crucial task of selecting a target market for a given product and designing an appropriate marketing mix (Tynan and Drayton, 1987, p. 301). It is one of the key building blocks of strategic marketing and is essential for marketing success. Highly successful firms make use of market segmentation (Lilien and Rangaswamy, 2003, p. 61), and it lies at the heart of successful marketing (McDonald, 2010). It also has one of the largest impacts on marketing decisions (Roberts et al., 2014, p. 127).

Market segmentation is a technique which can help firms find ways of establishing a competitive advantage. A market segment is a section of a market which possesses one or more unique features that both give it an identity and set it apart from other segments. Market segmentation amounts to partitioning a market into a number of distinct sections, using criteria which reflect different and distinctive purchasing motives and behaviour of customers. Segmentation makes it easier for firms to produce goods or services that fit closely with what people want.

Market segmentation research

Segmenting and selecting the optimum market segments are called target marketing. This is a vital marketing skill. Target marketing requires an ability to:

a   Find the key characteristic/s that break a market into relevant 'actionable' segments.
b   Identify and quantify which customers fall into which segments.
c   Target the best segments most likely to give the best results.

West (2010) suggests the critical things to look for are that it is large enough, has sufficient purchasing power, and is reachable. The organization should also be able to serve the segment effectively and target it with marketing programs.

One can segment consumer markets using many different variables including:

- *Geographic:* segments mean location, and this can include streets, towns, cities, regions, countries, continents, trading blocs like the European Union and NAFTA.
- *Demographics* or social statistics: includes age, sex, family, life cycle, job type/socioeconomic and group income level.
- *Geodemographics:* mixes geographic and demographic data to create categories of house types and locations – for example, people who live in detached houses in exclusive suburbs.
- *Psychographics:* attempts to segment according to psychological profiles of people in terms of their lifestyles, attitudes and personalities – for example, active go-getters.
- *Behavioural:* addresses behaviour patterns which include usage (e.g. heavy or light users) and uses, the ways a product or service is used – in other words, the benefit enjoyed.

Industrial, organizational or business-to-business markets can also be broken into segments and the most appropriate ones selected as target markets. Different variables are used for these types of markets: customer type, size, location, how they operate or the corporate culture. Customer type categorizes the type of product or service which the customer organization produces. In the UK, industry type is defined by the SIC, Standard Industrial Classification code. The size of the customer in terms of sales, number of staff and usage may determine whether it is worth targeting or not. Size of customer is also influenced by whether they are heavy or light users of a particular product or service and whether they are very loyal to a particular competitor.

Segmentation strategy

Some firms place a product within a single market segment. Few resources or a lack of competitors in the segment may make this strategy attractive. In so doing a firm may be able to develop a strong market position through gaining an in-depth knowledge of the segment's needs over a long period of time. Operating economies may also be obtained through specialization. Such a strategy is of course risky since a downturn in the market or the sudden emergence of a strong competitor can have a drastic impact on profits. A more conservative strategy is to look for a match between capabilities and the demands of several different segments. This makes it possible to spread the risk so that if one segment starts to become unprofitable there are still others that can bring in cash for the firm.

Firms sometimes concentrate on producing one product or service which is supplied to several different customer groups. In pursuing this strategy, a firm can build a good reputation in the area of the specific product. This also can be a risky strategy since it involves concentrating on a single product or service.

Concentrating on serving the needs of a particular group of customers represents yet another way of segmenting the market. This can involve making available many different products or services. Risk in this case is associated with a downturn in the fortunes of the particular group of customers selected.

Segment synergies

Firms which decide to serve more than one segment need to pay close attention to synergies between segments with respect to cost, performance and technology. Two or more segments might provide just the opportunity for exploitation because they share common distribution channels, manufacturing facilities, etc. The joint effect of marketing to all segments creates synergy. That is, the overall effect of marketing to two or more segments is to produce greater sales and profits than if each segment had been exploited one at a time in complete isolation from the others.

In international markets it is sometimes a good strategy to use a segment to which one can gain access as a stepping stone to other segments which may be difficult to access unless one already has a base in the country concerned.

Market targeting and positioning

A target market is the market or market segment which forms the focus of the firm's marketing efforts. Once segments have been identified, decisions about how many and which customer groups to target must be made. The options include:

> *Mass marketing strategy:* offering one product/service concept to most of the market across many market segments. Although scale economies can be achieved, there is a risk that few customers will be adequately satisfied. The underlying assumption of this approach, referred to as undifferentiated marketing, is that all customers in the market have similar needs and wants. It is argued that they can

therefore be satisfied with a single marketing mix – that is a standard product or service, similar price levels, one method of distribution and a promotional mix which is directed at everyone.

There are probably only two conditions under which a mass marketing approach is the most appropriate. The first reflects the demand side of the equation and is the position where there is little variation in the needs of consumers for a given product or service. This is a situation which is becoming increasingly rare, since in both consumer and industrial markets different individuals and organizations have widely varying characteristics, wants, needs and interests. The second condition reflects the supply side of the equation and refers to the ability of the enterprise to develop and sustain a single marketing mix that satisfies all. Where markets are large, this capability requires the availability of substantial resources.

More prevalent strategies are those which take account of the wide variation in customer wants, needs, characteristics and interests. For example:

Single segment strategy: concentrating on a single segment with a product/service concept. This is a relatively cheap option to use in terms of utilizing resources, but there is a risk of putting all the eggs in one basket – if the segment fails the company's financial strength will decline rapidly. Rolex, for example, targets relatively high-income consumers with its prestigious wristwatches. When world economies are buoyant sales will be good, but in times of economic recession even the better off can change their spending patterns.

There is also a problem with regard to flexibility in changing the product-market posture. High-quality image companies experience difficulty in terms of moving into product-market segments which have a lower-quality image. On the other hand, a single segment strategy does permit a firm to specialize, and the firm can concentrate all its energies on satisfying the wants of a particular market segment.

Multi-segment strategy: targeting a different product or service concept at each of a number of segments and developing a marketing mix strategy for each of the selected segments. Although this approach can spread the risk of being over-committed in one area, it can be extremely resource demanding.

Which target segment strategy a company adopts will be dependent on a wide range of market, product and competitive factors. Each of these must be carefully considered before a decision is made about segments to be targeted.

Factors influencing choice of targeting strategy

Having looked at some of the ways of targeting, let us now consider the kind of factors which influence choice of strategy.

Stage of product-market maturity: Segmentation strategies are most critical during the maturity stage of the product market, because buyers' needs are different. At the introductory stage of the life cycle there are few, if any, product-type competitors; however, competition can occur among alternative product types. If product-type substitution exists, the new market entrant may benefit from targeting one or more segments in the existing product markets. Where there are no product-type substitutes, a broad or relatively undifferentiated targeting strategy may be appropriate at the introductory stage of the life cycle. This may amount to attempting to identify a broad segment of potential buyers. The nature and intensity of competition at each stage of the product life cycle are important in guiding market targeting decisions.

Extent of buyer differentiation: When buyer wants are similar throughout the product market, there is less opportunity for extensive segmentation than there is in markets with buyers with different wants. A product market made up of a relatively small number of end-users is more suitable for a broad or relatively undifferentiated targeting strategy, particularly if the value of purchases of individual buyers is small. In addition, the more complex that the product-market structure is with respect to competing firms, variety of product-market offerings, variations in user needs and wants etc., the more likely it is that a useful method of segmentation can be found.

Market position: A firm's market share in an existing product market plays an important role in determining the target market strategy that it uses. Low market share firms have to compete in segments where their strengths are most highly valued and where large competitors are unlikely to compete. The strength may be in the type and range of products that are offered, the method by which the product is produced, the cost and speed of distribution or the credit and service arrangements. In these firms, management has to spend time identifying and exploiting unique segments rather than attempting to serve entire industries.

Structure and intensity of competition: When several firms are competing in an industry, selective targeting is often an appropriate strategy. Such selectivity is often essential for small firms in fragmented, transitional and global industries. Large firms may be able to reap the benefits of extensive targeting using a multiple-segmentation strategy.

Adequate resources: The possession of considerable resources can often place an organization in a position where it can consider various target market alternatives. Where resources are limited, however, a company may be forced to adopt a single-segment targeting strategy. The ability to analyze market capabilities is a decided asset, particularly where the task of market segmentation is a complex one. Thus, possessing both resources and the capacity to undertake such complex analyses provides firms with flexibility in choosing market targets.

Production and marketing scale economies: Choice of target market strategy may be influenced by production and marketing scale economies. The production process, for example, may require large-scale output to achieve necessary cost advantages. The same may also apply to marketing and distribution programs. In such cases an extensive market coverage strategy may be required in order to gain the sales volume necessary to support large-volume production and distribution.

Choice of segment(s)

Five factors govern the attractiveness of a segment (Doyle, 1994):

* segment size,
* current and potential competition,
* segment growth,
* capabilities of the business and
* profitability of the segment.

Deciding whether or not to enter a particular segment depends essentially on the match between the companies' capabilities and the characteristics of the segment. Although a large, expanding and lucrative market segment must be intuitively appealing, it will attract considerable competition, so a firm must have the capabilities (resources) to compete effectively in such a market segment. Similarly, as segments contract, larger competitors may tend to withdraw, making the segment less competitive and more attractive to firms with lesser capabilities.

Having looked at market targeting, we will now move on to look at positioning.

Positioning

Positioning, it has been suggested, represents the most important decision and action that management has to take for the company and its marketing, and yet it remains one of the most nebulous and controversial areas of new product development. Targeting and positioning strategies are interrelated. The choice of one or more target markets is based, at least in part, on the feasibility of the organization designing and implementing an effective positioning strategy to meet the target's needs. Positioning strategies used to pursue target markets may vary considerably, or they may have common features. For example, a firm may have a unique combination of the product offering, distribution approach, price, advertising and personal selling to serve each segment. Alternatively, some marketing mix components may be similar for different segments.

What is it that differentiates one product or service from another, even when they are almost identical? The answer seems to reflect the way in which the marketers of the product or service position them in the minds of users. Positioning refers to the decisions and activities intended to create and maintain a firm's product concept in customers' minds. Market positioning amounts to arranging for a product or service to occupy a clear, distinctive and desirable place – relative to competing products – in the minds of target customers.

What is being marketed must be perceived by the selected target customers to have a distinct image, relative to competitors, which meets with their own desires/expectations. The position of an offering is related to the attributes ascribed to it by consumers. These might be such attributes as its standing; its quality and the type of people who use it; its strengths, weaknesses and any other unusual and memorable characteristics it may possess; its price; and the value it represents to users.

The whole of the marketing mix is important in developing effective positioning, as attributes of the offering must be closely in line with the targeted customers' expectations and needs, as must the associated price points and channels of distribution. However, promotional activity is one of the fundamental elements of creating an effective positioning, as it is through promotion that the positioning is communicated to the target audience.

Positioning concepts

The positioning concept may be functional, symbolic or experiential. The *functional* concept is relevant to products designed to solve consumption-related problems for externally generated consumption needs. Toothpastes aiming to prevent cavities and banks offering convenient service fall into this category. The *symbolic* concept relates to the buyer's internally generated need for self-enhancement, role position, group membership or ego satisfaction. Cosmetics relating to life-style and clothes stressing image or appropriateness of occasion are examples of this. The *experiential* concept is used to position products that provide sensory pleasure, variety or cognitive stimulation. Documentary films and books are examples of this.

Corporate positioning

A more recent development has been the recognition that positioning is not just a matter between the brand owner and customers, but between the brand owner and every one of its stakeholders. The task has become one of deciding what is to be positioned and among whom it is to be positioned. In general terms, the solutions fall in two categories. In the first, it is the traditional view where a product, a marketing mix and a brand have to be positioned among the targeted customers. In the second, it is the *soul* of the entire organization – all-inclusive of its partners up and down the value chain – which has to be positioned among all the stakeholders of an organization. The second, more recent, view reflects that positioning is developing into an integrative construct which depends upon and affects every individual in the organization.

Brand positioning is a process of emphasizing the brand's distinctive and motivating attributes in the light of competition. Positioning refers both to the product segment the brand belongs to and how it differs specifically from other brands in the segment.

Positioning is becoming the universal strategic preoccupation of entire organizations and the concern of top management. In a business environment of continuous flux, it is more important to build corporate level strategic processes that facilitate dynamic repositioning than it is to build any defensible position. In the pursuit of this, organizations engage in 'patching'. This is the strategic process by which the business is routinely remapped to changing market opportunities.

Questions

1   What benefits are to be gained from employing market segmentation as opposed to treating the market as a single entity? Why should some bases of segmentation be more suitable for some products than others?

2   What factors impact upon a firm's selection of market segments? What do you understand by 'segment strategies', and how do these influence a firm's approach to market segmentation?

3   What do you understand by a competitive positioning strategy? How is product or service positioning accomplished? Discuss the factors that influence choice of positioning strategy.

4   What is repositioning, and why are products and services repositioned periodically?

5   How would you evaluate competitive advantage based on positioning analysis?

References

Doyle, P. (1994), *Marketing Management and Strategy*, Hemel Hempstead: Prentice Hall, p. 90.

Lilien, G.L. and Rangaswamy, A. (2003), *Marketing Engineering: Computer-Assisted Marketing Analysis and Planning*, 2nd edition, Upper Saddle River: Prentice Hall.

McDonald, M. (2010), 'Existentialism: A School of Thought Based on a Conception of the Absurdity of the Universe', *International Journal of Marketing Research*, 5(4): 427–430.

Roberts, J., Kayande, U. and Stremersch, S. (2014), 'From Academic Research to Marketing Practice: Exploring the Marketing Science Value Chain', *International Journal of Research in Marketing*, 31(2): 127–140.

Tynan, A.C. and Drayton, J. (1987), 'Market Segmentation', *Journal of Marketing Management*, 2(3): 301–335.

West, D., Ford, J. and Ibrahim, E. (2010), *Strategic Marketing: Creating Competitive Advantage*, 2nd edition, Oxford: Oxford University Press.

Further reading

Brotspies, H. and Weinstein, A. (2019), 'Rethinking Business Segmentation: A Conceptual Model and Strategic Insights', *Journal of Strategic Marketing*, 27(2): 164–176.

Dibb, S. and Simkin, L. (2001), 'Market Segmentation: Diagnosing and Treating the Barriers', *Industrial Marketing Management*, 30(8): 609–625.

Hooley, G., Nicoulaud, B., Piercy, N. and Rudd, J. (2017), *Marketing Strategy and Competitive Positioning*, 6th edition, Harlow: FT-Prentice-Hall.

Morgan, R.E., Strong, C.A. and McGuinness, T. (2003), 'Product-Market Positioning and Prospector Strategy: An Analysis of Strategic Patterns from the Resource-Based Perspective', *European Journal of Marketing*, 37(10): 1409–1439.

Sausen, K., Tomczak, T. and Herrmann, A. (2005), 'Development of a Taxonomy of Strategic Market Segmentation: A Framework for Bridging the Implementation Gap between Normative Segmentation and Business Practice', *Journal of Strategic Marketing*, 13(3): 151–173.

Weinstein, A. (2006), 'A Strategic Framework for Defining and Segmenting Markets', *Journal of Strategic Marketing*, 14(2): 115–127.

9   Marketing mix strategy

Marketing mix

Product, price, place, promotion, participants, physical evidence and process are the 7 P's of the marketing mix. McCarthy (1960) was the first to suggest the 4 P's of the marketing mix, though Wolfe and Crotts (2011), Riaz and Tanveer (n.d.) and Durmaz (2011) have indicated that Neil Borden coined the term 'marketing mix' in 1953. Cengiz and Yayla (2007) and Wolfe and Crotts (2011), citing some studies, asserted that McCarthy (1960) was the first to suggest the 4 P's as the primary ingredients of a marketing strategy, and as a means of translating marketing planning into practice, Rafiq and Ahmed (1995) quoted the following definitions of marketing mix: 'Marketing mix is a combination of all of the factors at the command of a marketing manager to satisfy the target market'. Booms and Bitner's suggested the 7 P's model (Booms and Bitner, 1981) which argued that the traditional 4 P's need to be modified for services include participants, physical evidence and process.

The product as a complex entity

The products or services of an organization help to create the image of the organization in the mind of the customer. This image is reflected in the customers' perceptions and feelings about its products or services. People purchase products and services to satisfy needs or wants and obtain benefits as a result. Organizations have to communicate these benefits to the user, directly or indirectly, in order to persuade the latter to make a purchase.

Product mix

Except in the case of very small firms, it is rare to find a firm offering a single product or service. It is much more common to find firms offering a mix of products or services. The product mix has:

- width – quantity of lines the firm carries, for example, radios, TVs, video recorders etc.;
- length – quantity of items in the product mix, for example, three kinds of radio and four kinds of TV;
- depth – number of variants of each product offered in the line, for example, clock radios, car radios, pocket radios etc.; and
- consistency – how closely related the various product lines are in terms of the use to which they are put, for example, all electrical leisure/ entertainment goods.

This provides a basis for defining the company's product strategy, since the company can increase its business in four ways.

1   New lines can be added to widen the product mix.
2   The length of existing product lines can be increased by introducing additional items.
3   New product variants can be added to deepen the product mix.
4   Product consistency can be made more or less depending upon whether a firm wants to acquire a strong reputation in a few or many different areas.

Product-line decisions

Attention needs to be paid to what competitors are offering. Gaps in the product line may become apparent when product offerings are compared with those of competitors. If a product line is too short, a firm may be able to increase its profits by adding items to the line. On the other hand, if it is too long, profitability may be improved by dropping products. There is a tendency for product lines to grow longer over time. When a product line is reviewed for its profitability, it may become apparent that profits can be improved substantially by pruning less profitable or unprofitable products and shortening the line.

Distribution strategy

There are six basic channel decisions to make. These are:

1   *Whether to distribute direct to the customer or indirectly through middlemen*
    The advantages of going direct are that it enables firms to exercise more control over marketing activities and it reduces the amount of time spent in the channel. The disadvantages are that it is difficult

to obtain widespread distribution and more resources are required to maintain distribution.

2   *Whether to adopt single or multiple channels of distribution*
The advantage of using a single channel is that it guarantees a minimum level of sales. On the other hand, the disadvantage of using exclusivity is that it does limit sales. In contrast, the use of multiple channels should lead to increased sales and a potential for wider distribution.

3   *How long the channel of distribution should be*
In determining the best channel length to adopt, the following factors have to be taken into account:

a   The financial strength of the producer – those in a strong position can carry out the functions provided by intermediaries.

b   Size and completeness of the product line – the costs of carrying out the distribution function can be spread across the various items in the product line. The more items, the more economical it might be to consider a shorter distribution channel.

c   The average order size – large orders may be distributed direct to customers.

d   The geographical concentration of customers – geographically dispersed customers merit a longer distribution channel because servicing them requires substantial investment of resources.

e   The distance of the distributor from the market – geographical distance makes it less attractive for the producer to want to supply direct.

4   *The types of intermediaries to use*
This involves choosing between different types of retailer in the case of consumer goods, for example supermarkets as opposed to cash and carry, and different types of distributor in the case of industrial goods, for example whether to use franchised dealerships or not.

5   *The number of distributors to use at each level*
In principle, more distributors are required if:

a   The unit value of the product is low and/or the physical quantity of stock held is likely to be high.

b   The product is purchased frequently.

c   There is a high degree of technological complexity in the product.

d   The service requirement is high.

e   The inventory investment is high.

f   Geographic concentration is low.

g   Total market potential is high.

h   The market share of the producer is high.

i   Competition is intense.

6   *Which intermediaries to use*
This is a qualitative decision and reflects whether the image of the particular outlet, the way in which it performs and the deals which can be struck with the distributor are satisfactory.

There are:

Vertical marketing systems in which channel activities are integrated and managed by one member of the channel – either a manufacturer, intermediary or retailer. Such systems reduce cost, minimize conflict among channel members, and build on the experience and expertise of channel members.

Horizontal marketing systems where strategic alliances and networks facilitate the development of horizontal marketing systems. They reflect the readiness of two or more autonomous units, who may even be competitors, at the same level in a channel to cooperate. Co-operation reduces the risks for an individual firm. It facilitates access to other channels of distribution, thereby accelerating market penetration. Moreover, it provides access to new technologies and know-how.

Multi-channel marketing systems in which different channels have emerged to meet customers' expectations. Although a multichannel marketing system provides the opportunity for a firm to serve a range of segments, it is a potential source of channel conflict. A producer has therefore to guard against the problems that this can create by being seen to be as fair as possible in dealing with channel members.

Pricing decisions

There are market conditions under which organizations can exert some control over the level at which price is set. If an organization cannot exert any control over the setting of pricing, then it has to accept whatever the market determines will be the price. We have to distinguish between a cost-oriented approach – based solely on a knowledge of a firm's own costs – and those which also take into account the demands of the marketplace. Economic theory argues that price balances supply and the demand for goods and services in the marketplace along with the 'law of demand' to explain this phenomenon. The law of demand purports that the quantity demanded per period of time is inversely related to price. Price elasticity of demand is a key concept. This is defined as the ratio of the percentage change in demand to a percentage change in price. Knowing the price elasticity of demand for its products or services can help a firm to set its prices. Estimating the price elasticity of demand can be more difficult, and the other variables may well have an impact on demand.

Cost plus approach: Many businesses simply work out the fixed and variable costs of the products or services they sell and add on a margin for profit. In doing so they may run the risk of setting the price too high or too low and not maximize their profits.

Demand-oriented pricing: A demand-oriented approach to pricing takes account of the strength of demand. Firms ask a high price when or where demand is strong and a low price when or where demand is weak, even if there is no dissimilarity in costs in either case. Differences in the strength of demand in the market enable firms to charge different prices in different market segments. The ability to practice this kind of price discrimination requires:

- different levels of demand in market segments,
- inability of buyers to resell at a higher price,
- that competitors will NOT undersell the firm in the segment being charged the higher price,
- cost of segmenting and policing the market to not exceed the extra revenue obtained,
- that price discrimination is legally permissible and
- that customers who pay more do not react negatively.

Such an approach is commonly referred to as charging what the market will bear.

Marginal pricing: Where a firm can recover its fixed costs in one market (a) for a product, it may be able to sell the same product in another market (b) at a much lower price provided the two markets are not in communication with one another. The price to be charged to the company (b) need only take account of the variable costs and additional transportation and delivery costs. And the firm will still be generating profit!

Penetration versus skimming pricing strategies: Penetration and skimming policies are most often encountered when dealing with new products, but they are sometimes used in other situations.

1   *Penetration strategy:* When introducing a new product, the objective may be to achieve early market penetration. The strategy may amount to setting a comparatively low price to instigate market growth and capture a large share of it. A penetration strategy may be appropriate if the market seems to be highly price sensitive, if a product is favoured

by economies of scale in production or where a low price discourages actual and potential competition.

2 *Skimming strategy:* A skimming strategy contrasts with a penetration strategy and is used to take advantage of the fact that some buyers are prepared to pay a much higher price because they want the product very much. Firms adopting this strategy may initially set a high price to gain a premium from such buyers and may only reduce it progressively to bring in the more price-elastic segments.

This strategy is appropriate where there exists a substantially large number of buyers whose demand is relatively inelastic. It may also be used where the unit production and distribution costs associated with producing a smaller volume are not so much higher that they cancel out the advantage of charging what some of the market will buy or where little danger exists that a high price will stimulate the emergence of competition.

Competition-oriented pricing: In this case, a firm makes sure that the prices it sets are in keeping with those charged by competitors, and it is often referred to as the going-rate price. In a purely competitive market, the firm exercises little choice in setting its price. In the case of pure oligopoly, it has more choice; firms can charge the same price as competitors. In view of the fact that there are only a few firms, each one of them knows the other's price, and buyers are also well abreast of prices.

Increasing prices without increasing prices

Organizations can often disguise price rises, permanent or temporary, by making it appear that no price rise is in fact occurring. This can be achieved in any one of the following ways:

1 The discount structure can be altered so that the total profit to the company is increased but the list price to customers remains the same.
2 The minimum order size is increased so that small orders are eliminated and overall costs thereby reduced.
3 Delivery and special services are charged for.
4 Invoices are raised for repairs on purchased equipment.
5 Engineering, installation and supervision are charged for.
6 Customers are made to pay for overtime required to get out rush orders.
7 Interest is collected on overdue accounts.
8 Lower margin models in the product line are eliminated and more profitable ones sold in their place.
9 Escalator clauses are built into bids for contracts.

10　The physical characteristics of the product are changed, for example, it is made smaller.

Price leadership strategy

This is the position where a particular supplier is generally accepted by other suppliers as the 'lead' firm in introducing changes in market prices. There are two principal forms of price leadership.

The first form of price leadership occurs when the largest firm in terms of market share – and/or the lowest-cost producer – leads on prices changes and other firms are prepared to follow because the price change yields them adequate profits. The second form, sometimes referred to as barometric price leadership, is where a particular firm, often a smaller firm, is 'adopted' as the price leader because it has demonstrated itself to be capable of spotting changes in market conditions.

In theory, a market leader enjoys all the advantages over competitors that are associated with higher volume sales. The leader should be able to set the price structure for the market. A market leader which takes a higher unit profit margin gives the whole market a form of price umbrella. Since all firms can charge higher prices, then profitability all round can be increased. This allows competitors to introduce product improvements funded by retained additional profits. Competitors can also invest in more aggressive marketing. The net result will probably be to weaken the market leader's position. Price leadership is often viewed by suppliers as a way of coordinating pricing policies so as to limit price competition and avoid the problems of price wars.

Marketing communications

There are a number of ways in which formal marketing communication can take place. These include different forms of advertising, personal selling and sales promotion. If more than one form of marketing communication is used, then there should be integrated marketing communication in the sense that they should express the same message. Choice of message and the method of communication adopted should reflect the objectives of the communication.

Marketing communication objectives

Marketing communications efforts can have different communications objectives. Some of these are listed here:

- to create awareness of a product or service,
- to provide information about a product or service,

- to generate enquiries,
- to build recognition of a company name,
- to reach those people who are beyond the reach of salesmen,
- to evoke desire for a product or service,
- to make the selling task easier,
- to overcome prejudices,
- to remind people about a product's benefits and
- to allay cognitive dissonance.

Designing the message

Effective communications have to appeal to the needs and wants of the recipients. They should give the recipient a motive or incentive to act. They also need to generate involvement with the message on the part of the recipient by asking questions which leave the message incomplete. In addition, they should also spell out exactly what course of action it is expected that the recipient will follow.

Messages can be built around rational, emotional or moral appeals, themes, ideas or unique selling propositions. Economy, value and performance are used in messages with a rational content. This type of message is often directed at industrial buyers and consumers making expensive purchase items such as cars, houses and substantial consumer durables.

Emotional appeals make use of both positive and negative themes. On the negative side this can involve fear, guilt and shame, whereas on the positive side it may comprise humor, love, pride and joy. Too much fear in a message may cause the audience to reject it. The use of humor may generate 'noise' and interfere with the message.

Moral appeals are attractive to people's sense of what is right and just. They can be used in 'green' advertising or in promoting social causes or even in things for children, for example, books and safety prams.

Media decisions

Organizations seek to discover the most cost-effective way to deliver the desired number of exposures to the target audience. This involves examining the reach, frequency and impact of advertisements that are placed in different media.

The size and composition of the target market and the cost of reaching that audience are indicators of the effectiveness of the media and are studied carefully by planners. In addition, circulation and type of audience are important measures taken into account by the planners. Other considerations are the quality of the editorials and the extent to which people pay attention to the advertisements.

A firm can vary its advertising expenditure to suit the seasonal pattern, or it can advertise throughout the year. Steady advertising expenditure should be used when habitual purchase patterns are greatest. More continuous advertising should be used when the rate at which new customers appear in the market is high. This should also be the case when the frequency with which people make purchases is high or the rate at which people 'forget the brand' is high.

Selling

Selling can influence any or all of the various stages in the purchase decision-making process. Selling is time consuming and a relatively slow way of influencing the purchase process. Where it is possible to achieve the same effect with other promotional tools, such as advertising, for example, selling will not be preferred since it will not be more cost effective in terms of time and money. However, it is possible to use selling as a marketing communications tool in niche market situations where advertising would be wasteful. The amount of marketing effort that firms put into personal selling varies according to the types of goods and services that are on offer. Industrial goods manufacturers put a greater financial emphasis on selling in the marketing mix, whereas large consumer goods producers tend to spend more on other forms of promotion.

Sales promotion

Sales promotions include special offers, competitions, price deals, trading stamps, trial offers, free samples, coupons, free gifts, in-store demonstrations and retailer discounts. They offer consumers the chance to get more than they expected and at the same time reduce the risk associated with buying. For example, product sampling affords the consumers the opportunity to try the product without actually buying it. Moreover, in terms of providing motivation to purchase, an extra discount or rebate means that the consumer is more likely to buy a product.

Marketing mix and the use of the Internet

E-marketing is the result of information technology applied to marketing. Successful online marketers exploit the interactive capabilities of the World Wide Web for the benefit of their customers. The web pages they create become communities where people swap information and buy regularly.

The World Wide Web can help foster brand identity and loyalty and develop long-term relationships with customers. Marketers can also advertise their products on the web sites of other organizations. This is found in the form of *banner ads*, which are small, static or animated rectangular ads that typically appear at the top of a web page. Users can click on the banners to visit the advertiser's site for more information. Finally, *sponsorship* or *co-branded ads* integrate companies' brands and products with the editorial content of certain web sites. Their role is to link the advertiser with the web site's mission in the user's mind.

An added advantage is that consumers can gain ready access to prices. This helps customers in comparative shopping and gives manufacturers that want to make price a key element in their marketing mix another opportunity to get pricing information to customers. Many organizations implement low-price policies through the Internet.

Total integration of the marketing mix

The various elements of the marketing mix effectively promote the image of the product in the customer's mind. The decisions taken with regard to the elements of the marketing mix should be in harmony with one another. Substantial deviation from what the customer might expect may sometimes have a negative effect on the customer's decision to make a purchase.

Questions

1   Discuss the importance of the price quality relationship in formulating marketing strategies.
2   What does the term strategy mean in the context of channel management?
3   How might the accuracy of communication be influenced by noise or distortion which enters into both the message and the channel?
4   Suggest some of the kinds of objectives that might be set for marketing communications. How might these objectives be pursued in practice?
5   Three important marketing communication tools are advertising, selling and sales promotion. To what extent are they:

a   complementary?
b   mutually exclusive as promotional tools?

References

Booms, B.H. and Bitner, M.J. (1981), 'Marketing Strategies and Organisation Structures for Service Firms', In J. Donnelly and W.R. George (eds.), *Marketing of Services*, Chicago, IL: American Marketing Association.

Cengiz, E. and Yayla, H.E. (2007), 'The Effect of Marketing Mix on Positive Word of Mouth Communication: Evidence from Accounting Offices in Turkey', *Innovative Marketing*, 3(4): 74–86.

Durmaz, Y. (2011), 'A Theoretical Approach to the Concept of Advertising in Marketing', *International Journal of Economics Research*, 2(6): 46–50.

McCarthy, E.J. (1960), *Basic Marketing*, Homewood, Ill.: Richard D. Irwin.

Wolfe, M.J., Sr. and Crotts, J.C. (2011), 'Marketing Mix Modelling for the Tourism Industry: A Best Practices Approach', *International Journal of Tourism Sciences*, 11(1): 1–15.

Further reading

Constantinides, E. (2006), 'The Marketing Mix Revisited: Towards the 21st Century Marketing', *Journal of Marketing Management*, 22(2–3): 407–438.

Harvey, M.G., Lusch, R.F. and Cavarkapa, B. (2015), 'A Marketing Mix for the 21st Century', *Journal of Marketing Theory and Practice*, 4(4): 1–15.

Long, T.V., Nguyen, J.C., Lu, V.N. and Hill, S.R. (2016), 'Engagement in Online Communities: Implications for Consumer Price Perceptions', *Journal of Strategic Marketing*, 24(3–4): 241–260.

Patil, D.D. and Bach, C. (2017), 'Marketing Mix for Strategy Building', *Journal of Multidisciplinary Engineering Science and Technology*, 4(4): 7146–7149.

Proctor, T. and Kitchen, P.J. (2015), 'Marketing Communications in a Post-Modern World', *Journal of Business Strategy*, 36(5): 34–42.

Sing, M. (2012), 'Marketing Mix of 4P'S for Competitive Advantage', *Journal of Business and Management*, 3(6): 40–45.

10 International marketing

Reasons for firms engaging in international marketing

Some firms prefer to supply goods or services just to their domestic markets if these are large enough to produce the kinds of financial returns they desire. For such firms there would not then be a need to learn another country's language and laws, deal with volatile currencies, face political and legal uncertainties, or design their products to suit different customer needs and expectations. As a result, business negotiations would be much easier to conduct.

However, there are several reasons why a firm might decide to become involved in international marketing operations. In the first place, foreign competitors offering superior products or lower prices might attack the company's domestic market. The firm might want to counterattack these competitors in their home markets to tie up their resources. Another point is that the firm might discover that some foreign markets present higher profit opportunities than the domestic market. Under such circumstances, even if there were risks and additional effort and resources required to secure business, it might be deemed worthwhile. Many firms also seek to grow sales and recognize the benefits to be gained from economies of scale. In the pursuit of such an objective a firm might need a larger customer base to achieve economies of scale and see additional sales in international markets as a means of achieving this end. A further reason might be that while there is additional risk involved in operating internationally, a firm may wish to reduce its dependence on any one market so as to reduce risk arising from such over-reliance on a domestic market.

International market entry methods

Once a company decides to become involved in international marketing it has to decide upon an approach. There are five broad market-entry strategies: indirect exporting, direct exporting, licensing, joint ventures and direct investment.

Indirect export: Here, firms work through independent intermediaries to export their products. There are four types of intermediaries:

- A domestic-based export merchant who buys the manufacture's products and then sells them abroad.
- A domestic-based export agent who seeks and negotiates foreign purchases and is paid a commission.
- A cooperative organization which conducts exporting activities on behalf of several producers and is under their administrative control.
- An export-management company which agrees to manage a company's export activities for a fee.

Direct export: In this case, firms can decide to handle their own exports. The investment and risks are greater, but so as the potential return as a result of not paying an intermediary. There are several approaches, and these can be made through the mechanism of:

- A domestic-based export department or division where there is an export sales manager and a team of sales people who carry out the actual selling and draw on market assistance as needed.
- An overseas sales branch or subsidiary which allows the firm to achieve greater presence and program control in a foreign market.
- Travelling export sales representatives where the firm can send home-based sales representatives abroad, where they will operate in much the same way as they do in the domestic market.
- Foreign-based distributors or agents where the company hires foreign-based distributors or agents to sell its goods on its behalf.
- Direct sales and marketing via the World Wide Web.

Licensing: This is a simple and relatively low-risk way for a firm to become involved in international marketing. The licensor licenses a foreign company to use a manufacturing process, trademark, patent, trade secret, or other item of value for a fee or a loyalty. The licensor in this way achieves entry into the market at little risk; the licensee gains production expertise or a well-known product or name without having to start from scratch. This is an approach which may be preferred where there is high monetary inflation or political instability in a country.

Joint ventures: Foreign investors may join with local investors to create a joint venture in which they share ownership and control. Forming a joint venture might be necessary or desirable for economic or political reasons. The exporting firm may lack the financial, physical and managerial resources to undertake the venture alone.

Direct investment: One form of foreign investment is the direct ownership of a foreign-based assembly/manufacturing or service facility. The would-be international marketer can buy part or all of a local company or even build its own facilities. As a company becomes more experienced in exports, and if the foreign market is large enough, then foreign production/ marketing or service provision facilities can offer significant advantages. For example, a firm can secure cost economies in the form of cheaper labour or raw materials. It can also gain a better image in the host country because it creates jobs.

The amount a company needs to invest varies with the degree of control it requires and the degree of risk it will encounter in entering a foreign market. It is often the case that the higher the degree of investment, the higher the degree of risk is. This is particularly the case if the company is attempting to enter the market alone.

Sometimes firms enter international markets with the co-operation of other firms already operating in the market. Developing strategic alliances and licensing agreements can allow entry to an international market which would otherwise have been expensive or very difficult to enter.

The most appropriate entry method to a new market is dependent upon various considerations. These include the extent of the company's existing international operations, nature of competition in the market, the potential barriers to entry, the degree of control required by the company, the availability of financial resources and the company's objectives in wishing to enter the market

Marketing mix strategy for international markets

Firms that operate in one or more foreign market must decide how much to adapt their marketing mix to local conditions. They can either standardize the product, advertising and distribution channels to produce the lowest costs because it involves no major changes to the domestic market or adjust the marketing mix elements to each target market.

In the case of using an adaptation marketing strategy, it will be necessary to consider the following adaptations:

> *Product adaptation:* This involves altering or adjusting the product or service to meet local conditions or preferences. This may also mean adapting to local superstitions or beliefs, too.
> *Promotion adaptation:* Firms can use the same promotion campaigns used in the domestic market but adapt them for each local market.

However, the use of media will require international adaptation because media availability varies from country to country.

Price: Prices of products and services usually differ across countries. The increased costs of transport, supplies, taxes, tariffs and other expenses that are necessary to adjust a company's operations to international marketing can raise prices. However, firms do have to be competitive and match offerings from other foreign competitors and home producers.

Place: Across countries, the nature of channels of distribution vary considerably. There are differences with regard to the number and types of intermediaries (e.g. product wholesalers, regional wholesalers, retailers) serving each foreign market. Another difference refers to the size and character of retail units abroad. Getting distribution for a product is a key to successful marketing operations and a thorough understanding of distribution channels and how they function is of paramount importance.

Developing an internationalization strategy

In order to operate beyond the bounds of its domestic market, an organization needs to internationalize its core business strategy. Choice of markets in which to operate is the first item on the agenda, and initial matters include identifying the market attractiveness of different options, assessing potential competition and studying ways in which to adapt to local conditions. Taking into account how to adapt products and programs to respond to foreign needs, preferences, culture, language, climate etc. is essential. One also has to consider barriers to trade, such as import tariffs and quotas and foreign ownership rules, as well as differences from the home country in laws, language, tastes and behaviour.

Internationalization can bring with it disadvantages, and in order to overcome the disadvantages it creates, companies need to adopt a globalization strategy that aids their search for a competitive advantage in world markets. Firms need to systematically analyze industry conditions and appreciate how they can best take advantage of the situations that exist. Market, cost, government and competitive drivers influence the industry conditions that affect competing with a global strategy. Market drivers relate to customer behaviour, the structure of distribution channels and the nature of marketing in the industry. Cost drivers relate to the economics of the business. Government drivers are set by the decisions laid down by national governments. Competitive drivers are produced by competitors' strategies.

Employing a global marketing strategy implies that a consistent marketing approach is used across different countries, although a small amount of latitude is allowed in terms of varying the marketing mix. Whether a product or service can be globally marketed depends on the extent to which usage of the product or service is rooted in national traditions. For example, the marketing of household cleaning products is rooted in traditional concepts of the role of homemaking. As these roles often differ considerably from country to country, there is often little scope for transferability of advertising that depends on such roles. On the other hand, products and services not influenced by national culture permit transferable advertising/marketing messages and themes. By and large this applies for most businesses to business products and services and also many newer consumer products and services, such as fast food and electronic entertainment goods (Festa et al., 2017).

Using a global positioning strategy and marketing mix

Using a common global positioning strategy can strengthen the effectiveness of a marketing programme since it has been tried and tested in many countries. Nevertheless, differences in the business's competitive position, purchase motivation and use/consumption patterns may strengthen the case for differing positioning strategies. However, firms that use a common positioning often find that they can make a large part of the marketing mix globally uniform.

Global brand names facilitate building global recognition for the product or service. In addition, combining a globally standard umbrella name with a local product name can be advantageous. The appeal of a global brand name is partly related to the global acceptance or prestige of the home country of the brand name, how important it is to have a name that means something and how easy the name is to pronounce. Brand names that mean something usually need to be translated in order to carry out the positioning job for which they were intended.

Having a global price is seldom possible because of international differences in market price levels and other factors influencing price. A useful strategy is to try to set the prices relative to competitors in each market.

Global advertising can be varied in a number of ways:

- Use the same copy – here a product, service or brand is positioned in the same way making the same claims.
- Use the same script – the advertising employs the same script in different countries, but the actual execution is different. Being able to use a common script depends largely on the universality of the images chosen and of the situations and characters to be used, and also the need for differentiation from local competitors.

- Use the identical advertisement – in each country the same advertisement is used and only the voices or text are translated.

Some companies use two types of campaign for different purposes – first, a globally uniform campaign which sets out the main theme and then local campaigns for tactical purposes.

There are advantages and disadvantages to globalization (Smith and Clinton, 2016).

Conditions where a global marketing approach may be most useful

A firm may benefit more from applying global marketing in larger countries. In this case cost reduction, improved programme effectiveness, enhanced customer preference, and increased competitive leverage can be more significant. However, larger markets can be more challenging from the point of view of local adaptation than smaller markets. Customers in smaller countries are more accustomed to products and programs that are not specifically adapted for them and are usually subject to more cultural influence from larger neighbours.

Disadvantages of adopting a global strategy

Globalization has its disadvantages. For instance, it can lead to increased management costs through increased coordination, reporting requirements, and manpower. It can also decrease management effectiveness if over-centralization adversely affects local motivation and morale. Product standardization can produce a product or service that fully satisfies no one.

Analysing international marketing opportunities

With the exception of marketing through export houses in the domestic market, producers know where their goods are going. The need to understand the export marketplace in the same way as they understand the domestic marketplace is therefore very important.

In particular, a firm should establish stated foreign government policies about the range and type of imports that will be accepted into their countries and the extent to which those foreign governments impose tariffs and quotas to protect industry at home. In addition, international marketing is a complex business, and there are legal and financial regulations to understand. Furthermore, the marketing and commercial infrastructures of countries differ considerably, and it is important to understand these since they will have a strong impact on marketing operations.

It is very important to understand the drivers of consumer behaviour in foreign markets and the extent to which they differ from the domestic market and other foreign markets. We cannot assume that what we hold to be true of the home market necessarily remains true when we consider different foreign markets. Life cycle patterns, bases of motivation, cultural values and lifestyles may be very different from what we are used to and require an entirely different marketing approach.

Marketing communication channels need to be explored to identify how effectively information regarding products and services can be brought to the attention of the consumer. Literacy and language are often difficult barriers that have to be overcome.

Most important of all as far as the firm is concerned is the capacity of the market to pay for the goods and services supplied. This will be influences by such factors as personal disposable income and government restrictions on the expenditure of foreign currency reserves. For larger items and industrial projects loan terms, interest and capital requirements are also key factors (Chandra et al., 2009).

Using the World Wide Web

Arguably, Internet marketing capabilities enhance the firm's ability to generate other internal capabilities within the firm, which in turn have a positive impact on the international market growth of the firm (Mathews et al., 2016).

While the Internet brings goods to the screens of very geographically distant customers, the same distance creates difficulties in returning unsatisfactory goods and in many cases even the payment for such goods. Although credit cards facilitate intercontinental transactions, people are reluctant to give out their credit card numbers over the Internet for reasons of security, as mentioned earlier. The alternative ways of paying for goods are often too daunting for the uninitiated user of such mechanisms.

Firms doing business with customers in other countries have to be aware of the laws that apply when promoting their goods and services over the Internet. This is more of a problem for some goods and services than for others. In addition, in the online community there is a general feeling that unsolicited e-mail is unacceptable. Organizations need to be wary of considering such approaches in order to induce dialogue with consumers. Such approaches may even incur legal action.

However, the Internet is an important source of communication for marketers and customers alike. In order to get the best out of website marketing, organizations need to understand how the potential customers are making use of the web. Users of the web tend to surf or skim its contents, so would-be marketers need to find something with immediate appeal to potential customers. The site needs to be updated regularly, as well, and information given as to the changes that have taken place.

Questions

1   The idea of international marketing is an outmoded concept. All markets are international in nature, and the concept of international marketing is spurious. Discuss.
2   Globalization has changed the whole nature of marketing. There are no longer national markets of any significance. To what extent would you agree or disagree with this point of view? Explain.
3   What should firms that operate in one or more foreign market take into consideration when deciding how much to adapt their marketing mix to local conditions?
4   Discuss the advantages and disadvantages of the World Wide Web as a vehicle for marketing goods and services.
5   What do you see as the future of e-marketing? How might it develop and impact on our lives in the next 30 years?

References

Chandra, Y., Styles, C. and Wilkinson, I. (2009), 'The Recognition of First Time International Entrepreneurial Opportunities', *International Marketing Review*, 26(1): 30–61.

Festa, G., Ciasullo, M.V., Vrontis, D. and Thrassou, A. (2017), 'Cooperating for Competing: A Small Italian Wineries' Internationalisation Strategy Case Study', *Global Business and Economics Review*, 19(5): 648–670.

Mathews, S., Bianchi, C., Perks, K.J., Healy, M. and Wickramasekera, R. (2016), 'Internet Marketing Capabilities and International Market Growth', *International Business Review*, 25(4): 820–830.

Smith, A.D. and Clinton, S.R. (2016), 'Globalisation within a Rich e-Commerce Environment: A Case Study of Large Manufacturing Firms', *International Journal of Business Information Systems*, 22(4): 436–454.

Further reading

Chaffey, D. and Ellis-Chadwick, F. (2015), *Digital Marketing: Strategy, Implementation and Practice*, 6th edition, Harlow: Pearson.

Crick, D. and Crick, J. (2016), 'The First Export Order: A Marketing Innovation Revisited', *Journal of Strategic Marketing*, 24(2): 77–89.

Dominici, G. (2009), 'From Marketing Mix to E-Marketing Mix: A Literature Overview and Classification', *Journal of Business and Management*, 4(9): 17–24.

Doole, I. and Lowe, R. (2004), *International Marketing Strategy*, London: Thomson Learning.

Frost, R., Fox, A.K. and Strauss, J. (2019), *E-Marketing*, London: Routledge, p. 6.

Martin, C. (2013), *Mobile Influence: The New Power of the Consumer*, Basingstoke: Palgrave Macmillan.

Schellenberg, M., Harker, M.J. and Jafari, A. (2018), 'International Market Entry Mode: A Systematic Literature Review', *Journal of Strategic Marketing*, 26(7): 601–627.

Zhang, J. and Zhu, M. (2016), 'Market Orientation, Product Innovation and Export Performance: Evidence from Chinese Manufacturers', *Journal of Strategic Marketing*, 24(5): 377–397.

11 Marketing planning and implementing marketing strategy

Introduction

Marketing planning is a logical sequence and a series of activities leading to the setting of marketing objectives and the formulation of plans to achieve them (McDonald and Wilson, 2011, p. 24). The marketing plan is linked to the corporate plan of the business in which the company operates, indicates financial objectives that have to be accomplished, specifies how revenues are to be generated through various marketing programs and assesses the various costs that will be incurred in achieving these objectives.

The corporate plan answers the questions:

- Where are we now?
- Where do we want to go?
- How do we organize resources to get there?

A marketing audit amounts to an evaluation and assessment of all factors which affect the firm's marketing performance. The factors can be internal to the firm or can be part of the external environment. The internal audit comprises a detailed analysis by product/service of the market share and profitability of the various lines. Strategies relating to marketing mix elements are reviewed and studied together making the use of marketing research data. An examination is also made of marketing budgets and how they were drawn up and related to previously set objectives. The external audit commences with a review of the general economy and makes an assessment of the prospects for the firm's markets. It estimates what should be the appropriate action taking into account economic and market indicators. Many factors have to be considered. Economic, fiscal, social, business, legal and technological developments all have a substantial impact on the business. In addition, market segments, channels, products, end uses, needs, tastes, attitudes, stocks and profits also have to be taken into account.

Attention also has to be paid to the activities of competitors and potential competitors.

Gap analysis

Figure 11.1 shows the concept of gap analysis.

Forecasting what is likely to happen in each business sector in the immediate and longer-term future is necessary. The organization must make predictions that take into account factors which are external to the firm such as market trends, economic trends, competitive trends, sociocultural trends and technological trends. The implications of these trends are then compared with the likely performance of the company based on internal factors such as product strengths, material costs, technical ability, productivity prospects and financial capacity.

The next step is to project earnings from existing business over the timescale of the forecasts and to make comparisons with the required objectives. The firm then has to examine its current position. It has to predict when the changes are likely to occur and what impacts these will have on its sales and profitability.

Predicted changes in technology often indicate the presence of a potential profit gap arising. That is a gap between what the firm wants to achieve in terms of profit and what it is likely to achieve on the basis of its existing portfolio of activities. Usually this will mean that there is a need to find ways of filling the profit gap by generating products and projects which will generate the required profit.

A firm has to relate the expected profit from any new ventures to the amount of resources employed to achieve that profit. The measure it needs

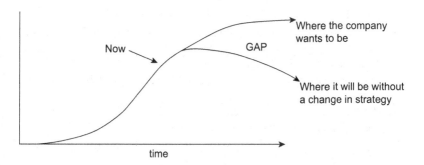

Diagram showing the gap between expected and required profits

Figure 11.1 Gap analysis

to consider is the return on investment generated by new actions it may take. Return on investment for individual products can be linked to the overall rate of return on capital employed earned by the business. Performance of the firm in the latter respect is reflected in the general confidence of other firms and financial institutions in dealing with the firm in the marketplace and in the firm's ability to attract and retain shareholders' investments.

As a rule, firms strive to maintain their existing rate of return on invested capital. In pursuit of such an objective they should only accept new projects which promise a return on investment potential which is at least equal to the current rate of return on capital employed. Of course, even then, as its more profitable offerings start to decline, firms may not be able to maintain the existing rate of return on invested capital.

In practice, of course, firms have to accept the best available projects. These may generate below the required rate of return, with an inevitable negative impact on medium/longer-term profitability.

Assessing company strengths/weaknesses and threats and opportunities in the environment – SWOT analysis and the TOWS matrix

SWOT analysis is a technique specifically designed to help with the identification of suitable business strategies for an organization to follow. It involves specifying and relating together organizational strengths and weaknesses and environmental opportunities and threats. In practice this is often an activity that is not carried out well. It is all too easy, having identified all the important points, not to know what to do with the data generated.

The TOWS matrix (Weihrich, 1982) presents a mechanism for facilitating the linkages between company strengths/weaknesses and threats and opportunities in the environment. It also provides a framework for identifying and formulating strategies. Opportunities, threats, strengths and weaknesses have to be identified and listed in the matrix. Next, various combinations of opportunities and strengths, opportunities and weaknesses, threats and strengths, and weaknesses and threats are examined in order to generate possible strategies. The concept of the TOWS matrix is shown in Figure 11.2.

It should be observed that in generating strategies one seeks to maximize on strengths and opportunities and minimize on weaknesses and threats. Brainstorming may be used effectively in helping to identify factors and generate strategies.

Implementing the TOWS matrix requires that the following steps are carried out:

	Strengths	Weaknesses
Opportunities	Maximize on strengths and opportunities	Maximize on opportunities, minimize on weaknesses
Threats	Maximize on strengths minimize on threats	Maximize on weaknesses, minimize on threats

Figure 11.2 The TOWS matrix

1 Pinpoint and assess the impact of environmental factors – economic, political, demographic, products and technology, market and competition – on the organization.
2 Make a prognosis about the future.
3 Undertake an assessment of 'strengths and weaknesses' in terms of management and organization, operations, finance and marketing.
4 Develop strategy options.

Working systematically through this process enables internal and external factors to be entered on a grid and different combinations to be studied. For example, the entry to one cell of the grid could involve maximizing opportunities and maximizing strengths. This would amount to putting together at least one strength and one opportunity to produce a strategy that capitalizes upon this combination. Figure 11.3 illustrates the TOWS MATRIX being used by a maker of plastic bin liners seeking to generate strategies.

The marketing plan

The final step involves developing the marketing plan so that objectives which have been identified and decided upon can be systematically pursued. The plan will vary from organization to organization and situation to situation. However, the composition of the overall marketing plan is such that it is built up from separate sub-plans. These would include such things as a *product* mix plan, sales plan, an advertising plan and a sales promotion plan. Other sub-plans could include physical distribution, market research and research and development, pricing and even regional plans.

THE TOWS MATRIX

Product: Plastic Bags

	Strengths	*Weaknesses*
	1 Brand name	1 Exports
	2 Distribution	2 Sales force
Opportunities	3 Low costs	
1 Need for robust rubbish disposal bag	Use existing distribution and brand name to market scented bin-liners (S1, S2, O3)	Strengthen sales force and export skills, look at European markets (W1, W2, O2)
2 European markets		
3 Scented bin-liners		
Threats	Capitalize on brand name, distribution and low costs to meet competition from imports (S1, S2, S3, T2)	Develop capability in substitute materials particularly for products that can be sold to export markets (T1, W1)
1. Substitute matrials		
2 Imports		

Figure 11.3 Example of TOWS matrix

Note: In Figure 11.3, S1,S2,S3 denote the organization's indicated strengths, W1,W2,W3 its weaknesses, T1,T2,T3 the threats and O1,O2,O3 the opportunities in the marketplace.

Formulating the plans

With the exception of advertising and certain expense items, goals need to be established by region, district and the salesperson's territory. Territory goals should be undertaken jointly by the salesperson and his or her manager. Sales goals are then broken down by weeks, taking into account seasonal variations. These then become budgeted figures against which subsequent performance is measured.

At the next stage, strategy and tactics feature predominantly. Strategy selection involves working out the best way to attain specific objectives. Tactics appertain to the specific action that must be taken, by whom it should be taken, when and within what constraints. Taken together they specify how the plan is to be put into effect.

Control procedures are incorporated into a plan and are concerned with specifying those measures in the organization which have to be monitored to assess how well a plan is succeeding. Control establishes the standards, measures the activities and results, compares the measurements with the standards and reports variances between the measurements and the standards. This enables a plan to be kept on course and facilitates the kind of decisions that need to be made with regard to modifying the original plan if need arises.

Contingency planning is undertaken to specify what action will be taken if key objectives cannot be accomplished subsequent to implementing the plan. One must also be on the lookout for cases where achievements greatly exceed planned expectations.

Although there is no absolute prescription for the format of a marketing plan, the following provides an indication of a suitable layout.

1 *The executive summary:* The plan should commence with a summary of the main objectives and recommendations. Such a summary allows the reader to get to grips with the major thrust of the plan. Following the executive summary there should be a table of contents for the planning document.

2 *The current marketing situation:* This might comprise five sections:

    a *The market situation*
       In this case data may be made available concerning the target market. It may consist of the size and growth of the market and trends that are taking place. Data might be shown for several years and certainly for all the different market segments – geographic and otherwise. Data might also be presented on identified customer needs and buying behaviour.

    b *The product situation*
       In this case a breakdown of sales, prices, contribution margins and net profits for each of the major product lines over the past few years is required. Actual data might show such things as industry sales, company market share, average price per unit, variable cost per unit, gross contribution per unit, sales volume, sales revenue, gross contribution margin, overhead, net contribution margin, advertising and promotion expenditure, sales force and distribution expenditure, marketing research expenditure and net operating profit.

    c *The competitive situation*
       The purpose of this section is identifying the major competitors, their size, goals, market share, product quality, marketing strategies and any other characteristics that are needed to understand their intentions and behaviour.

    d *The distribution situation*
       Data indicating the size and importance of any new channels of distribution should be shown in this section, along with any developments or trends in distribution methods.

e   *The macro-environment situation*
This section should provide data on relevant broad macro-environment trends that have a direct bearing on each product line's prospects for the future. The trends might include demographic, economic, technological, political and sociocultural factors.

3   *Opportunity and issue analysis:* Here the main opportunities and threats in the environment, strengths and weaknesses of the organization and issues facing product lines might be identified.

a   *Opportunities and threats analysis*
This is the part of the SWOT or TOWS analysis which identifies opportunities and threats facing the organization with respect to the product lines.

b   *Strengths and weaknesses analysis*
This is the part of the SWOT or TOWS analysis which looks at the strengths and weaknesses of the product lines.

c   *Issues analysis*
Here the organization has to review the findings of the analysis so far in order to come up with key questions or issues that must be addressed in the marketing plan. Issues might relate to questions such as whether the organization should stay in its current business; whether it can compete effectively; and whether it should maintain its existing marketing mix policies.

4   *Objectives:* The next part of the planning document might relate to the financial and marketing objectives that the organization wants each of its business units to achieve.

a   *Financial objectives*
In this case, return on investment aspirations, net profits and cash flow figures need to be provided for each of the product lines.

b   *Marketing objectives*
Financial objectives have to be expressed in terms of marketing objectives.

5   *Marketing strategy:* The marketing plan might be structured along the following or similar lines:

a   Specify the target market.
b   Indicate how the product is to be positioned in the minds of the customers.
c   Indicate how the product line is to be changed by the addition/deletion of product offerings.

d   Indicate the pricing strategy or strategies to be adopted.

e   Indicate how effort is to be expended to improve or change levels of distribution.

f   Show how the sales force is to be motivated, compensated or altered in strength in order to sustain the new selling effort.

g   Show how service levels are to be maintained, improved or curtailed in order to facilitate the achievement of the plan's objectives.

h   Indicate the nature of the advertising campaign that is going to help achieve the increase in level of consumer awareness etc. that will eventually lead to increased market share achievement.

i   Indicate how the sales promotion is to be changed in order to stimulate consumer purchases at the point of sale.

j   Indicate how the R&D budget is to be altered to enable the market share to be sustained in the long term through the introduction of new products and new models.

k   Indicate what is to be spent on marketing research to improve knowledge of consumer wants and needs and to monitor competitor moves.

6   *Plan of action:* The points outlined in the previous section represent the broad strategic plan that is necessary to achieve the company's objectives. In this next stage, each marketing strategy element has now to be elaborated to show:

- what will be done,
- when it will be done,
- who will do it and
- how much it will cost.

7   *Projections of profits and losses:* The action plan will enable the marketing manager to develop a budget requirement. On the revenue side it will show predicted sales volume in units and the average realized price. On the expense side, it will show production costs, physical distribution costs and other marketing costs broken down into fine detail. It will also show the projected profit based on these figures.

8   *Controls:* The final section of the planning document should outline the nature of the controls to be employed in monitoring the progress of the plan when it is put into operation. This section of the plan might also contain contingency plans. Such plans would outline what action would be required as a response to specific adverse developments which might have a profound effect on the achievement of what has been set out in the budget.

Next, we introduce the notion that strategic windows offer possibilities for opportunities to be shared with other organizations where it is of mutual interest to co-operate. Even the traditional idea of competition may be sacrificed in favour of collaboration and co-operation if the circumstances are right and it is mutually beneficial to all concerned.

Strategic collaboration

Rapidly changing markets, new technologies and a shortage of skills and resources have made firms think in terms of building relationships with other companies so that together they can present a more powerful front. This has led to a shift from an emphasis on competition to an emphasis on strategic collaboration. The latter varies ranging from vertical channel relationships and supplier/manufacturer collaboration to horizontal relationships in the form of strategic alliances and joint ventures.

The new organizational forms resulting from collaborative relationships with customers, suppliers, distributors and even competitors are referred to as networks. In these kinds of organizational structures, marketing and other business functions are carried out by different independent organizations and individuals. Many networks have been created in the service sector, and networks spanning complexes of supply chains have also begun to develop. Networks can be complex in nature and are often controlled and directed by management information and decision support systems which perform many of the command and global functions of the traditional organization. As a result, networks tend to be flexible and adaptable to change. The relationships among the firms in a network can include simple transactional contracts of the conventional buyer-seller type; supplier-producer collaborative agreements; strategic alliances or partnerships; consortia; franchising; and joint ventures (Kanter, 1994).

Alliances and partnerships

One can visualize collaborative business relationships in terms of a spectrum running from transactional relationships to complete vertical integration. At one end of the spectrum, a firm brings in goods and services from outside as an alternative to producing them internally. It might go outside for services such as advertising, marketing research and direct marketing. At the other end is the fully vertically integrated firm which does very little or no outsourcing at all. In between there are a number of different kinds of collaborative arrangements (Koza and Lewin, 2000).

Partnerships are alliances between organizations, some of which may have a short-term focus and involve limited co-ordination, whereas others have a longer-term focus and move beyond co-ordination to integration of activities. Yet another type of partnership may be an arrangement viewed as permanent where each party views the other as an extension of its own firm.

Joint ventures are alliances where the ownership of a project or operation is shared between the parties concerned. Some joint ventures focus on partners from different industries sharing innovative design abilities, technological expertise and marketing capabilities to innovate.

Vertical integration is where an activity is fully owned by the core organization, although the relationship may still be seen as a strategic alliance.

Strategic alliances: management issues

Collaboration and partnerships permit each organization to focus on its own core competencies and to benefit from the specialization of other organizations in their own area of expertise. Clarity in defining core competencies is essential, and this can sometimes be difficult to do. Failure to accomplish this can undermine the purpose of the alliance. Choice of partners is critical, and one has to take account of whether an environment of trust, commitment and co-operation between the members of the alliance is likely to occur (Humphries and Wilding, 2004).

Relationship marketing

Relationship marketing brings long-term financial benefits to an organization. It is a means to an end and is based upon two economic arguments. First, it is more expensive to win a new customer than it is to keep an existing customer. Second, the longer the association between the company and the customer, the more profitable the relationship for the firm should be.

Relationship marketing evolves ties between the organization and its customers to improve feedback and develop customer loyalty. Customers are open to the pressures of competitive promotions and may readily switch brands or store, so a firm needs to establish a stronger relationship with customers. Relationship marketing tries to get customers to actively support the firm and its products and to encourage others to do the same. The aim of relationship marketing is to find ways of enhancing the mutual benefits derived from the relationship. Successful relationship marketing involves the targeting of customers of sufficient value to justify the investment in creating a relationship with them. Relationship-building resources can be directed to those customer groups where this is mutually advantageous. The strongest relationships are based on the establishment of mutual trust and respect between organizations concerned (Grönroos, 1997).

Questions

1 What are the advantages of strategic alliances and networks over previously used methods of gaining access to new products, new markets and more diversified activities?
2 What do you regard as the key issues that need to be assessed when considering strategic alliances?
3 Is relationship marketing really any different to any other form of marketing? Why do you think it has come into fashion at the present time?
4 Given the nature of a rapidly changing environment where new developments take place very rapidly and firms need to react rapidly, is the idea of planning ahead still relevant? Why or why not?
5 Illustrate how the TOWS matrix might be used in an organization of your choice. Evaluate its usefulness in the context of the strategic planning process.

References

Grönroos, C. (1997), 'Keynote Paper From Marketing Mix to Relationship Marketing: Towards a Paradigm Shift in Marketing', *Management Decision*, 35(4): 322–339.

Humphries, A.S. and Wilding, R. (2004), 'Long Term Collaborative Relationships: The Impact of Trust and Behavior', *Journal of Marketing Management*, 20(9–10): 1107–1122.

Kanter, R.M. (1994), 'Collaborative Advantage', *Harvard Business Review*, 72(4): 96–108.

Koza, M. and Lewin, A. (2000), 'Managing Partnerships and Strategic Alliances: Raising the Odds of Success', *European Management Journal*, 16(2): 146–151.

McDonald, M. and Wilson, H. (2011), *Marketing Plans: How to Prepare Them, How to Use Them*, Hoboken: Wiley.

Weihrich, H. (1982), 'The TOWS Matrix: A Tool for Situational Analysis', *Long Range Planning*, 15(2): 54–66.

Further reading

Anslinger, P., and Jenk, J. (2004), 'Creating Successful Alliances', *Journal of Business Strategy*, 25(2): 18–22.

Buchel, B. (2002), 'Joint Venture Development: Driving Forces towards Equilibrium', *Journal of World Business*, 37(3): 199–207.

Day, G.S. (2003), 'Creating a Superior Customer-Relating Capability', *MIT Sloan Management Review*, 44(3): 77–82.

Gibbs, R. and Humphries, A. (2009), *Strategic Alliance and Marketing Partnerships: Gaining Competitive Advantage through Collaboration and Partnership*, London: Kogan Page.

McDonald, M. and Wilson, H. (2016), *Marketing Plans: How to Prepare Them, How to Profit from Them*, 8th edition, Chichester: John Wiley.

Wright, E., Hillon, Y., Garrido-Lopez, M. and Fowler, D. (2019), 'A New Scorecard for Strategic Planning', *Journal of Business Strategy*, 40(2): 50–58.

Index

Note: Page numbers in *italics* indicate a figure on the corresponding page.

Printed in the United States
by Baker & Taylor Publisher Services